FUNNY THING, GETTING OLDER

About the Author

Michael Morpurgo has written more than 100 books and has won the Smarties Prize, the Whitbread Award, and the Blue Peter Book Award. He is the author of *Private Peaceful*, *Kensuke's Kingdom* and *War Horse*, which has been made into a Tony Award-winning Broadway play and a Golden Globe-nominated film. He was Children's Laureate from 2003–2005, a role that took him across Britain to inspire a love of reading in children.

Michael and his wife Clare founded Farms for City Children in 1976 at Nethercott Farm in Devon, and Michael has called the project his 'greatest story'. They aim to expand the horizons of children from towns and cities all over the country by offering them a week in the countryside living together on one of their farms.

[signature]

SIGNED BY THE AUTHOR

MICHAEL MORPURGO

FUNNY THING, GETTING OLDER

and other reflections

hodder press

First published in Great Britain in 2025 by Hodder Press
An imprint of Hodder & Stoughton Limited
An Hachette UK company

The authorised representative in the EEA is Hachette Ireland, 8 Castlecourt Centre, Dublin 15, D15 XTP3, Ireland (email: info@hbgi.ie)

1

Copyright © Michael Morpurgo 2025

The right of Michael Morpurgo to be identified as the Author of the Work has been asserted by him in accordance with the Copyright, Designs and Patents Act 1988.

The sources for individual pieces can be found on pp.313–314.

All rights reserved. No part of this publication may be reproduced, stored in a retrieval system, or transmitted, in any form or by any means without the prior written permission of the publisher, nor be otherwise circulated in any form of binding or cover other than that in which it is published and without a similar condition being imposed on the subsequent purchaser.

All characters in the play extract in 'The Voices of Children' and the story excerpts in 'Will There Be Singing?' (*I Believe in Unicorns*), 'Perchance to Dream' (*Our Tree of Hope*) and 'A Letter from Grandpa Christmas' are fictitious and any resemblance to real persons, living or dead, is purely coincidental.

A CIP catalogue record for this title is available from the British Library

Hardback ISBN 9781399739719
Trade Paperback ISBN 9781399739726
ebook ISBN 9781399739733

Typeset in Sabon MT by Hewer Text UK Ltd, Edinburgh
Printed and bound in Great Britain by Clays Ltd, Elcograf S.p.A.

Hodder & Stoughton policy is to use papers that are natural, renewable and recyclable products and made from wood grown in sustainable forests. The logging and manufacturing processes are expected to conform to the environmental regulations of the country of origin.

Hodder & Stoughton Limited
Carmelite House
50 Victoria Embankment
London EC4Y 0DZ

www.hodderpress.co.uk

This book is dedicated to Adele Armstrong, my producer on *A Point of View* on BBC Radio 4, who helped me gather my thoughts and inspired me to write many of the pieces.

CONTENTS

Preface ... 1

Childhood ... 11
Great Expectations ... 13
Owl or Pussycat? ... 18
The Happiest Days of Your Life ... 23
Let Me Take You There ... 30
Passing It On ... 39
All Around the Year ... 44
The Voices of Children ... 51
Little Amal ... 80
Set Our Children Free ... 86

Peace and War ... 115
Lucy Lost ... 117
The Tilth of Truth ... 128
Poppies ... 134
Imagine ... 138
The Road to Peace ... 144
The Phoenix of Peace ... 149
All the World's a Stage ... 158

FUNNY THING, GETTING OLDER

The Violin of Hope	164
Finding Alfie	170
A Strange Meeting in an Oxford Restaurant	180
Telling Tales	189
Will There Be Singing?	191
Perchance to Dream	209
Coram, Hogarth, Handel and Mozart	223
War Horse	229
Listen to the Children	243
Searching for Wonder	251
A Fine Night, and All's Well	253
Places of Wonder	264
Funny Thing, Getting Older	267
I Wonder. An Epitaph	272
The Boy Who Would Be King	280
Dawn Chorus	286
Taking Time	291
A Letter from Grandpa Christmas	299
Poems for Vivaldi's 'Four Seasons'	304
Sources	313
Endnotes	315
Index	317

PREFACE

In a sense, this preface is by way of being a postscript to my writing, my storytelling life: to my life. So it is both preface and postscript.

I'm older now. Not wiser maybe, but with perhaps the perspective that only old age can bring, on the world about me, on my place in it. And it is a funny thing, old age. I mean, you have to laugh and smile, or you'd just turn your face to the wall.

The essays and reflections in this book have been written over recent decades, many for BBC Radio 4's *A Point of View*, some as articles in newspapers and some as lectures. And woven in amongst them you will find a play, a poem or two, and even a few stories. I'm not abandoning storytelling.

Throughout my writing life I've largely written fiction, but I've been feeling for a while now that it's important also to explore other ways of 'passing it on', as Alan Bennett's wonderfully eccentric teacher tells his class in *The History Boys*. He's trying to tell them why he teaches, what he's here for, what we're all here for. It's what writing is for as well.

FUNNY THING, GETTING OLDER

I suppose this whole book is a way of being an explanation, or justification, or both. As a writer, I have moved, rather thinly disguised, through my stories, autobiography hidden in amongst the fiction, not very well concealed either. There are many Michaels in my stories, even the occasional Michael Morpurgo – perhaps a sign of a limited imagination. But the truth is that I have played out my life often in my fiction, using up the experiences and happenings of my 80-odd years. I write biographically, that's the truth of it. It's my memories that fuel much of my writing. I write more often than not in the first person, in order perhaps to live the story more intensely as I tell it. I've been me, often. I've been a horse, a dog, a cat, all sorts. I've been old, I've been young. I've been girl, I've been boy. After all, 'One man in his time plays many parts.'

But maybe there comes a time to stand back, to try to see the world more clearly, as I find it, and to tell it straight – not through the prism of a story, but to look my reader in the eye and come clean about the real world, the great issues of our times: caring for the planet, peace, migration, fairness, education, hope. Now that I'm 80, it seemed the time to do it, the time not to play a part, while there is time.

I am very fortunate to be getting older and still to be doing work I love. One of the great joys is when people – young

PREFACE

people especially – suggest to me that I might like to write or do something different, something I haven't dared do before. Maybe they read my books when they were children, or their own children read them now, maybe I taught them at school.

As with this book, they nudge me into believing I can go where I have not gone before, and that is hugely exciting. Would you like to write for radio, an essay for *A Point of View*? Would you like to write a series of poems for Vivaldi's 'Four Seasons' and then read them at a concert? Would you write an article for a newspaper on education, on peace and war, on migration? Would you like to narrate the story of *War Horse* to accompany the music from the National Theatre's play at the Proms? Or, would you like to gather a selection of your writings together for a different kind of book altogether, this book?

Simply to be asked is great encouragement and so heartening – especially when you're 80-plus. They must think I can still do these things and do them well enough. That's all I need to launch into something new. So here it is. When I thought of calling this book *Funny Thing, Getting Older*, I had very good reason for suggesting that title. A story, a true story.

Heart bypass surgery is not funny. But recently I had to go through it. Not funny at all. But then a funny thing happened on the way to the operating theatre. I was wheeled into a sort of antechamber where I met the anaesthetist. She'd been to see me on the ward earlier to introduce herself and tell me how it was all going to be, that everything would be fine. She seemed very kind. Polish, she told me. I recall thinking she looked like a kind auntie of mine when I was little. 'I'll see you shortly,' she said. And off she went.

She was waiting for me in this antechamber, the theatre beyond it, with everyone waiting. She was dressed in white from head to toe, mask on. I knew the routine. She would make conversation to relax me and put me to sleep without my knowing it was happening. The conversation, which I knew sooner or later would be interrupted, went like this.

> Her: I heard that you are a writer.
> Me: Yes.
> Her: What sort of books do you write?
> [*She is going through the motions, I thought*]
> Me: Children's books, mostly.
> Her: And what's your latest book about?
> Me: [*Waiting for unconsciousness to overwhelm me*] A dog.
> Her: A dog! [*Suddenly seriously interested. No longer just going through the motions*] What kind of a dog?

PREFACE

Me: A corgi.
Her: A corgi! I've got a corgi! What kind of a corgi?
Me: A Pembrokeshire corgi.
Her: I've got a Pembrokeshire corgi! When's the book coming out? I want to come to the launch and bring my dog, my Rufus, along.

I'm sure I went off to sleep with a smile on my face. Several hours later, I woke up and we arranged it. It wasn't just talk. It wasn't going through the motions. So I will be sharing the launch of my next book with a Pembrokeshire corgi called Rufus and a Polish anaesthetist called Agatha. Apparently, she has many friends who have corgis. It could be quite a gathering! I hope the dogs behave!

As I said – funny thing, getting older.

—

I have just looked out of my window and seen what I often see at about 8.30 in the morning: a group of children from a city primary school going back down the lane for breakfast after a rainy walk out over the fields to feed the cattle their hay, to move the sheep onto new pasture. It's been bucketing down. Their hoods are up and they're dripping wet. They are linking arms and laughing too. And I'm thinking how lucky I am to witness at my age how positive young people can be, how together they are and happy about their work, in the fractured world we live in. Having my children and grandchildren about, seeing them and these city children down on the farm that we have turned into a charity to allow them to experience country life, always fills me with hope and joy, puts the world and its troubles, age and its drawbacks into perspective, keeps me smiling. *This is the generation*, I am thinking, I am hoping, *who will put things right*.

Funny thing, getting older. Well, not so funny for so many. Not funny for those living in isolation and with sadness in their hearts, not funny at all for those who are overwhelmed, or cold and hungry, for those worn down by ill health. Not funny for those living through war. Not funny when you lose those you love, friends and family, as inevitably happens in old age.

Living through war, as so many do the world over, is not simply seeing it on the television or reading about it – though that is bad enough. The constant drip, drip of horror – from the Middle East, from Ukraine, from Sudan, from so many places – invading our homes and our lives and our minds is corrosive to the soul, to our very humanity. The tragic drama of a world out of kilter, seemingly destroying itself, is playing out in front of our eyes from our phones and iPads and

PREFACE

televisions, from our newspapers. And we are helpless to do anything about it. Or so it might seem.

Not true, of course. We have voices and we can speak up. We can tell our stories, read the stories of others. We can write. We can do what we can do. We must. Generations before us did, and gave us our freedom to speak, gave us new hope. We have to do the same for the generation that just walked down the lane on the way back from their farm work. I feel in a way that this is mutual. They give me the hope to keep my pecker up, to keep me smiling though.

A story is like a kite. Every time I write or tell a story, I'm flying a kite. If I make it right, if the wind is right, if I design it right, if I fly it right, it will lift and rise and stay up. It will swoop and soar, and it will please my heart when it's up there, floating on the wind, flapping and rustling in the breeze. And it will please anyone who sees it. They will stop and stare and marvel at the sight of it up there in the blue. It may fall, catch in a tree, but I can rescue it, mend it and fly it again. It is same with the making of the stories in this book, every one of them, the poems and the essays too. I have to keep making and flying my kites, and teach others, if I can, to fly theirs.

Within this book you will find an account of why kites came to mean so much to me, how I came to write a book about the sheer joy of them. It reflects on why they are important to the child in me, the teacher in me, the story-maker in me, the old man in me. They are to me and to many cultures symbols of hope, of happiness, of peace and freedom. And the older I have become, the more I value all four, but the greatest of these is hope. Of all the stories I have written, that story – which became my book *The Kites Are Flying* – has become the one that stays in my mind more than any other, now especially. It is about children, about suffering and war, about reconciliation, about our longing and our hope for peace. And you will read about a visit I made to Gaza and to Israel some 20 years ago, and of the one place, the one school, where I felt a path to peace was being prepared. It was here I saw children, Jew and Arab together, making and flying kites.

I remember leaving at the end of my visit and thinking how different this school was from anywhere else I had visited, in Gaza or in Israel, how the children learnt together, played together, lived as neighbours side by side in the village. This must surely be the only way forward, through education in school and in the community, through hope and belief. In a place of such historic and bitter conflict, this has to be the pathway to peace. I thought then that perhaps the children who had made and flown the kites with me – given

PREFACE

half a chance – might be amongst the future peacemakers who would make it happen. That is still my hope and my belief all these years later.

I'm writing this on 7 October 2024, a year after the appalling tragedy in Israel and Gaza, and now in Lebanon, after a year of unimaginable horror for everyone living on both sides of the borders. I'm wondering still how many of those kite-making, laughing children are alive, and if so, where they are now, what they believe now. Have they lost all hope? I'm wondering if the story I told about them is too fanciful. I hope it's not. I do know that without hope, there is no hope. I have to keep hoping and believing, for the children and for me. What else can keep us going?

And we have reason to hope. All wars end in the end. I was born during a world war that was the most destructive war ever fought. The generation before me and our generation found a way afterwards to forgive, to forge friendship, to knock down walls. There is peace now in South Africa, on the island of Ireland – not perfect peace maybe, but peace. It can and will happen too in Israel and Gaza, and it will be the children on both sides who, with education, with knowledge and empathy and understanding, will do it. Maybe with the help of stories and kites, linking arms and laughing.

CHILDHOOD

GREAT EXPECTATIONS

2024

I saw the film of *Great Expectations*, in black and white, way back in the 1960s, at a family Christmas. It was a life-changing experience. It doesn't matter how many versions of the film I've seen, this is the one I remember. It doesn't matter how many family Christmases I've had – about 80 now – this is the family Christmas I remember best.

Let me set the scene. It is 1961. I am 18. I am home, rather unwillingly, for Christmas. Christmas was always a big deal in our family, too big a deal, with all the rather overdone tradition and ritual. We lived in a musty, dusty old house, where the floorboards creaked and where in winter the windows iced up inside. We always had many guests at Christmas. There was much jollity and playing of games – charades was a favourite. There was also some tension in the air – actually, the tension was in the family. It always was.

After the war, the divorce rate multiplied by four quite quickly. Collateral war damage, you could call it. My father was away in Baghdad in 1945 when he received a letter from my mother telling him she wanted to leave him and marry a man she had met and fallen in love with. I was two at the time, my brother four.

As soon as he could, my father – Tony Bridge he was called – came home on compassionate leave to try to persuade my mother not to leave him. He took her on a cycling holiday to Southwold where they had been happy together before the war. They were both actors, travelling the country 'in rep'.

Sadly, Tony's plan didn't work. My mother would not change her mind. She decided to leave, taking my brother Pieter and me with her. So we found ourselves growing up in a divorced family with a stepfather, one Jack Morpurgo, writer and publisher.

Divorce in middle-class England in those days was of course thought shameful. Pieter and I grew up with a new surname, Morpurgo, and soon had a half-brother and -sister. We were the Morpurgo family.

Pieter and I knew we had a different father, but his name was never mentioned. He became for us a phantom father, a hush-hush father. We never saw him. If ever we asked our mother about him, as over the years we increasingly did, she would simply refuse to tell us anything about him. 'That was then,' she would say. 'This is now. Let's not talk about it.'

GREAT EXPECTATIONS

Tony, our real father, had made the decision – we later learnt – that he didn't want to 'play' at being our father. Better for us growing up to have a new father, a new family, was the thinking, without a spare father hanging around. Having been abroad during most of the war, he hardly knew us and we did not know him at all.

Jobs in the theatre after the war were difficult to find, so he soon emigrated to Canada, where he found work and great success in Stratford, Ontario, and later in the Shaw Festival Theatre in Niagara. We never saw Tony. Pieter and I would fantasise about him sometimes, very privately.

By 1961, the family had our first television set. Two channels, black and white, and tiny. It took ages to warm up and flickered constantly, but it was a marvel! Like many families then, we all gathered round this new toy eagerly. My stepfather disapproved and rationed us. But, being literary, he did approve of dramatisations of Dickens on the BBC at teatime on Boxing Day.

So, with a supply of crumpets piled up on the dish, and keeping warm by the fire, we all settled down to watch *Great Expectations* – children, aunties, grandparents, all of us. I was sitting in the chair next to my mother, everyone in a state of great expectation. It's the best opening of any of Dickens' books. Pip, a young boy living out on the marshes, is taking a shortcut home through the village graveyard on his way home, the evening darkening around him. He is timorous and we are terrified.

Then, up from behind a gravestone rears a hideous figure and grabs him by the arm. Most of us know the story and we're waiting for the moment. It's Magwitch, the escaped convict, his chains rattling. He has wild eyes and a face like a wolf. The watching children scream. My mother gasps and grabs my hand. 'Oh my god,' she cries. 'It's your father, it's Tony!'

One or two step-relatives leave the room at once. The genie is out of the bottle. The phantom father is in the room! Soon, everyone leaves except my mother and Pieter and me. We watch in silence together. And I'm thinking, *That's my father?! My father is a very convincing convict! Does he really look like that?*

Two short postscripts
As for Tony, my father, Pieter and I met him in our twenties, became good friends with him and found our dad. I last saw him in Niagara, on the lake in Ontario, at the Shaw Festival. He was 80, still acting. I was there to see him in a play by Arthur Conan Doyle about the last surviving soldier from the Battle of Waterloo. A monologue at 80 and he was word perfect, pitch perfect.

GREAT EXPECTATIONS

The film of *Great Expectations* we saw that Boxing Day of 1961 might not have been the great David Lean one, but it was wonderfully done, and produced by the Canadian Broadcasting Company, in which Magwitch was of course played quite magnificently!

OWL OR PUSSYCAT?

2020

Written in lockdown, one of many tales of reflection.

This year, many thousands of families may have to do without the school Christmas play or panto or concert. And that's a pity, a real pity. It's a ritual much loved, very much part of the beginning of a family Christmas. It will be much missed. So I thought I'd tell you the story of how I acted in my school Christmas play when I was little, in 1949. It's a true story, promise.

My mother, Kippe Cammaerts, was an actor, as was my father, Tony Bridge. They both went to drama school at RADA. They got married soon after and acted together in the same company, touring the country in rep, from Southwold to Canterbury, from Bristol to Edinburgh. I should have followed in their footsteps. If I'd had the courage, and the talent, I would have done just that. I had my chance, my one big chance, and I blew it. I'm telling you, I could have been George Clooney.

This is how I blew it. It was the first time I ever acted on stage. I lived in Earl's Court in London and went to school

OWL OR PUSSYCAT?

down the road, at a primary school called St Cuthbert with St Matthias. It's still there. I've been there and read to the children, in the very same school hall where I had my starring role.

I was six, I think. I wasn't that keen on school. There were rules, spelling tests and punishments. There was detention if you were naughty, if your socks were down or if you were late for class; it was the ruler if you were very naughty, if you said a rude word or cheeked the teacher.

But I always liked the stories and poems our teacher read to us, and that was because my actress mother used to read to me and my elder brother, Pieter, every bedtime. She could be a pirate or a princess, a lion or an elephant. She was living the story, making music with the words, becoming the characters in front of our eyes.

She always had her favourite stories and poems, and amongst them was Edward Lear's *The Owl and the Pussycat*. I loved that poem so much that I used to echo the words with her every time she recited it. Then it happened by chance one day that our teacher read it to us in class. She said that the headteacher had decided to make it our school Christmas play to be performed in the school hall in front of all the parents and teachers.

A few days later, she made us come out one by one to read the poem in front of the class. The headteacher was there too, so we were all sitting up very straight. I couldn't read very well – I was slow that way – but I didn't need to read it at all. I simply stood up there and recited that poem by heart. I loved the rhythm of it, the fun of it. I did it without nerves and without any hesitation. I have never forgotten the look of amazement on our headteacher's face, on those faces all around me.

A day or two after that, she announced to the whole school at assembly that Michael Morpurgo would be playing Owl in the school Christmas play – the main part! After school I ran all the way home, burst in and told everyone the good news. They were over the moon. My auntie, I remember, cried with pride and joy.

The trouble came the next day when I found out who was to be Pussycat. It was Belinda, who was my secret girlfriend. To be clear, I was quite shy. She was older than me and I'd hardly spoken to her, let alone declared my love for her. Within a week or two, we were both in rehearsals, sitting there in the 'pea-green boat', and I was singing her a love song, strumming my pretend guitar, while the teacher played the piano and Belinda meowed loudly, caterwauling. Everyone laughed because she did it so well. But it rather spoilt my song. What no one understood, least of all Belinda, was that I meant every single word of my love song. So for me it was no laughing matter.

OWL OR PUSSYCAT?

They made the scenery, with a great big white balloon hanging above us, which was the moon. They put up the stage and the curtain in the school hall. We made the paper chain decorations and they brought in a huge Christmas tree and stood it up in the corner by the piano. They couldn't get the lights to work but that didn't matter.

The great day was coming, everyone was becoming very excited. I found I was getting rather nervous too. I lay in bed at night worrying. Would I remember my lines? Would I sing in tune?

My auntie and my mother made my owl costume. I was feathers all over, with claws and a beak and big pointed ears. I was so pleased with it. I opened my wings and ran around the house towitowooing. They all said I made a wonderful owl. But when I put it on for the first time at school for the dress rehearsal everyone laughed – except Belinda. She said I looked just right, like a proper owl. I loved her even more. And in her costume, with her whisker make-up and her long white tail, she looked more like a cat than any cat I ever saw. She even moved like a proper cat. And she caterwauled like a proper cat too. And she wasn't nervous at all. She was cool as a cucumber. I was in awe of her.

Then, at last, it was the last day at school before Christmas. The great day had arrived. The school hall was packed. The hum of the audience beyond the curtain was the most exciting sound I ever heard. And then the curtain opened ...

And I blew it.

—

Years later, when I was much older and had become a writer, when any hope of being George Clooney had long since faded, I sat down and wrote the story of that school Christmas play, in which I played the starring role opposite the love of my life. Luckily for me, it was illustrated beautifully by the wonderful Polly Dunbar and published in a book called *Owl or Pussycat?*

Read it and you can find out how I comprehensively blew my chance of a life on the stage or screen, how my career as an actor ended there and then in 1949, on that fateful stage at St Cuthbert with St Matthias Primary School.

And that's a pity. I could have been a contender!

THE HAPPIEST DAYS OF YOUR LIFE...
2019

For many they used to be, for many they still are. But for an ever-increasing number of young people today, childhood can be marred, scarred by mental illness, overshadowed by anxiety and stress. Some 10 per cent of children aged between 5 and 16 have a clinically diagnosable mental health problem.

Yet surely we are living in a gentler age for our children, kinder, with school and home and society itself more child-centred and sensitive, better informed. Or so we hope and believe. After all, gone are many of the strictures of punishment and fear that previous generations had to endure – the routine use of the cane in class, the strap at home. Childhood really should be the happiest days of our children's lives. For over a million of them today it is not. Depression, self-harm, eating disorders, attention deficit disorder, anxiety attacks. Poor mental health manifests itself in many ways.

Schools, teachers and parents, all of us, are bewildered and overwhelmed by what seems to be a rising epidemic amongst the young. There have to be underlying reasons why this is happening. We have to look at what is different now in our society that might be causing this. Is it that childhood itself has changed, or that society has changed, or both? I know the old days were not good old days. I was there. More children lived in abject poverty, childhood disease was more widespread, education and healthcare could be rudimentary, homes were often cold and damp, unemployment was rife and families were dysfunctional then too. And society was in turmoil, even trauma, in the post-war years when I grew up. There can be no doubt that many children were suffering in those times with mental health problems. But such problems were generally much less well understood then of course, and even if recognised would often have been unacknowledged or hidden away.

That said, childhood really was different then. Strangely, just after the war, with bombsites down the street and at the bottom of our school playground, with the shadow of war all around, with loss and grieving in almost every home including mine, there was, comparatively speaking, little anxiety in our lives. We played in those bombsites, made games out of war. We lived in the bubble of our family, our street, our school, our friends. There was a togetherness. Our parents and extended families kept us safe, protected us. But at the same time, they let us have our freedom. Recent research has shown that children then had nine times more time and space in which to play and wander and explore than they do now. Playing out was all there was to do. Football in the street, marbles or hopscotch on the pavement, climbing walls in the bombsite, making camps, bird nesting (yes, I know!), collecting beetles and worms. There was chess, and draughts, dominoes, and children's radio, and books and gramophone records.

Through this play, we made strong friends – in the family, on the street and in the playground. It was a secure world they made for us, a close-knit world where we felt we belonged. There was a structure there, a cast of familiar characters, a way of being we all shared and understood. We knew who was good: policemen (mostly), doctors, nurses, vicars, teachers (mostly), the milkman (and his horse), the postman, the coalman (and his horse). And we knew what was good too, and bad. School and home and church taught us that.

Essentially, it was a kind world. In such a society there was little anxiety amongst the children. There were teachers I feared and avoided as best I could. I didn't like to go to sleep in the dark. I had my fears. But they were fleeting fears. I grew up in a divorced family. But no one spoke of it at home.

FUNNY THING, GETTING OLDER

I am not saying that it was an ideal home or an ideal world for a child to grow up in. But I feel very strongly that I was fortunate to be a child in that time. As I see it, most children of today have to grow up fast, are confronted all too early with the complexities of modern life. The world is beamed directly into their bedrooms, though phones, iPads and computers. All too young, they can travel to the dark, troubling and incomprehensible places of the worst of human behaviour. They can meet who they like, talk to any stranger and discover online just what everyone is saying about them. They can read deeply hurtful, scathing personal comments that they know everyone else is reading too. And very often, they do all this in isolation. For many, modern technology inhibits talking, replaces play, limits human communication. This virtual world can be a maze of hideous nightmares, images and events, whether fact or fiction, that can breed fear and hurt and confusion in young minds, that can prove toxic for the children of today. Self-confidence and self-worth, the two great pillars of a child's sense of wellbeing, can so easily be destroyed.

But for a child to be unwanted, to be rejected by one parent or both, is the hardest cut of all, and one of the most likely circumstances to cause mental illness. Divorce, separation, family instability is much more common now than when I

THE HAPPIEST DAYS OF YOUR LIFE...

was little. The rate of divorce quadrupled after the Second World War. When a child is unwanted, abandoned, has no family to call her or his own and is given away into care, it is a wound that is difficult to heal. And we have to remember of course that it is the grown-up adult world that creates the world of the child. We bring them into the world, the world we have made. We ourselves are deeply damaged by anxiety, by stress. One in ten of us have at some stage been treated for some form of mental illness. Seventeen of us die by suicide every day in the UK. Many of us find it hard to cope, too hard to cope. Despair begins with anxiety. And despair takes a terrible toll.

So how specifically can we protect our children from the causes of this anxiety that can do so much harm? Parents and schools can and must control the exposure of young people to social media and to the darker, more pernicious parts of the internet. Children have to learn its immense benefits too, discover its potential for knowledge and understanding and good, and that takes time and maturity. It can be done. I know many parents who do it. Schools can do more, so much more, to alleviate stress amongst our children.

They are of course at school to learn, but they are at school also to grow, to play, to make friends, to discover themselves, to build that essential self-confidence and self-worth. But education policy for decades now has driven schools and teachers remorselessly, and overwhelmingly, towards teaching to the examination, where pupils, teachers and schools are judged on their academic success rate. Minority subjects are ditched, music and art and drama and dance and sport marginalised. Pass well and you are a success; pass ordinarily or fail and you are a failure. Whether passing or failing, you can be living through so much anxiety. And that can and does bring on mental illness in childhood, or indeed is the root cause of mental health breakdown later in life.

So first, let children enjoy being children at home or in playgroups for seven years, as already happens in other, more enlightened societies, and then let the priority in schools be to create the atmosphere and conditions where all children can flourish and find what it is they love to do and can do well. We have to inject into the lives of children such memorable happenings that will make them feel they belong. It is moments, days, people that change lives, that breathe into a child's life a new way of thinking, new hope, something to look forward to, something to look back on that they have loved. The making of joyous memories can help a child through hard times. A good book, a play, a piece of music, a

THE HAPPIEST DAYS OF YOUR LIFE...

visit to a museum or the countryside, a glimpse of a kingfisher flashing by, watching a calf being born, collecting a warm egg from under a hen, grooming a horse, scuffling through leaves down a country lane. Such moments are life affirming, they strengthen all of us, give us all heart and hope, a sense of wellbeing, of belonging.

LET ME TAKE YOU THERE

2020

I live in Devon, in the heart of the country, in a thatched cottage called Paradise, down 'deep lanes', as Ted Hughes called them. Our lane leads only to the River Torridge. Larks rise in the high field behind our house. Swallows and buzzards and bluebells greet us on our daily walk. But the cows and calves barely look up as we go by, they are so used to us. Otters and kingfishers are there somewhere by the river. We look for them but rarely see them. They know we are there, and we know they know we are there.

We all share this paradise on earth. Yet this paradise is not my place of dreams. I live here, see it out of my window, have lived here with our growing family, work here on the land, at my writing, for 45 years and more. I have no need to dream of home when I am home.

I dream, as so many do, of those I long for but cannot see. I dream of what is out of reach, places and faces I remember, times I remember. Places and times I can escape to only in dreams. But there is one place, and one time, that I dream of most often, most vividly. Maybe because I saw it first with a child's eye.

Childhood is rarely all sweetness and light, nor are dreams of childhood. Dream and nightmare are close companions. I grew up in grey, grim, post-war London. It was a place of grieving and sadness. Mornings when the smog was so yellow and thick you couldn't see across the street. School, to me, was fearful – so often the place where punishments happened. Standing in the corner, detention during playtime, the ruler on the hand stinging. Fear ruled.

And then, when I was about seven, the family moved out of the gloom of still bombed-out London to the Essex coast. To Bradwell-on-Sea, my place of dreams then and even now, in my older age, even in my pastoral paradise.

New Hall. The house where we lived was not new at all, but a rambling, spidery, draughty Tudor house, full of creaking corridors and attics with windows and doors that rattled in the wind, with great oak beams above and open fireplaces which filled the house with woodsmoke and very little heat. For heat, there were paraffin stoves that stank to high heaven but did warm hands. Feet got chilblains that itched and hurt at the same time. Then, joy of joys, we had a dog to play with. At last. A golden retriever we called Prynne, who was mad and disobedient and chased his tail, who stole food off the table and came up to our room and lay on our beds, which was forbidden and he knew it. We loved him to bits.

Pieter, my elder brother, and I had bedrooms right up in the attic. In summer, we could climb out of the window and sit there in the gully. This was our private world. The stairs were too steep for the 'little ones', our younger brother and sister. We were as high as the treetops, looking up at the stars and the moon, listening to the distant murmur of the sea and the hush of the wind in the trees. Owls would hoot at us and we would hoot back.

And we had a wilderness of a garden. Our own jungle. Here we found frogs and toads and snakes and birds' nests. Here we climbed trees, picked Bramley apples from the orchard to store in the old corrugated Nissen hut in the garden where the soldiers had lived during the war. We once found a rusty old tin mug they had left behind and a cigarette packet with a sailor's face on the front which I kept for years. And an old boot with snails in it. There was a rusty iron bed in a corner and above it a much-faded photo in a frame, hanging crooked on the wall. We thought it must be the king, and out of proper respect we didn't take him down.

In the tiled barn, which was leaning precariously, where the roof was sagging, where pigeons roosted and cooed, where swallows nested, Pieter and I played ping pong or marbles. Hide and seek too. The little ones joining in if we allowed them; I always cheated and looked through my fingers as I was counting to see where they were hiding.

There really was a spreading chestnut tree just outside the barn, with shiny conkers that we collected by the dozen, some as big as apples. And we played conkers for hours, late into the evening. Afterwards, there'd be hot chocolate at the kitchen table in our pyjamas, with a gramophone playing somewhere, loud. Often Mozart's horn concertos, I remember. His music often plays through my dreams. Then came a story, upstairs in our attic, that my mother would read and which was always over too soon. She'd kiss us, leaving us with just the scent of her. Once she'd gone, we were out of bed in a flash and dropping down into the gully outside our window to do our owl hooting.

We had kind and doting aunts, and both of us had been given bikes. Pieter a bright red one, mine was a smart green. Both Raleighs. We'd be out on them all we could, in sun and rain, the wind in our faces, cycling out past the school and the American air force base to the chapel near the sea wall. St Peter's it was called. Mr Dowsett, the builder, who we saw a lot of when he came in to keep the barn from falling down altogether, told us proudly that it was the oldest chapel in the whole country. Saxon, he told us, and he never told a lie. He said as much, more than once.

It was close to St Peter's that I saw my first hare, my first heron, my first kestrel, my first fox and, once, a deer. Or maybe I made that up. I made up a lot as a boy. Still do; never really grew out of it.

And there were larks rising over the fields, and housemartins, and swallows flying so low overhead, so close I thought they might get caught in my hair. We'd haul ourselves up onto the sea wall and would sometimes have to walk then, wheeling our bikes because the wind from the heaving brown North Sea gusted so hard that we'd be bound to fall off if we ever got on. We leant over the handles of our bikes into that wild wind as we pushed them along the sea wall, and it blew our breath away.

But even as we lost our hearts to this haven of a home there were storm clouds gathering. We were sent away to boarding school, miles away in Sussex. My mother said it would be fine, that the school was lovely, that it overlooked Ashdown Forest, where Christopher Robin and Pooh had played Poohsticks. That was no consolation to us. We were being ripped away from the place we loved, where, for a short time, our happiness had been complete.

This school too was ruled by fear. Fear of failure and the punishment that went with it. The slipper. The cane. We didn't see our home by the sea, or our bikes, or Prynne, or our family, for months on end. In my lumpy, squeaky bed, I dreamed of it. Longed for it. Longed for them.

But one holidays when we got home, we discovered the halcyon days were over, the spell broken. The village children who had always been fine and friendly towards us ostracised us. Living in the big house had always been something to be teased about, to live down. But now going away to a posh school had created a rift between them and us. That soon became aggressive. We were ambushed on bike rides. They called us names over the wall and threw sticks and stones. They all hurt. I still harboured my love of the place, but now we hunkered down more and more behind the wall that separated us from the village street and everyone we had known there. The chapel, the sea wall, our bike rides were becoming a memory. A dream. We fitted in nowhere.

The local farmer brought a hare one day for my mother. I watched him taking off his cap and handing it over. Holding it up triumphantly by its hind legs. Blood dripping from its nose. There was much talk that evening about how kind it was of him and how my mother was going to cook it. That it had to hang in the larder for a few days before being jugged. Horrified at the thought of this, I did a brave and a terrible thing. I crept into the larder late at night. There was this beautiful creature hanging from a hook in the ceiling. I took her down, went out into the garden and buried her deep in the soft soil beyond the corrugated iron Nissen hut.

When the crime was discovered the next morning, I suggested it must have been Prynne who had jumped up and carried the hare off. That the larder door must have been left open or something. I always thought that might have been the reason that Prynne was not there when I came home the next Christmas holidays. They'd decided that they couldn't cope with him, that he ran off too much. That he jumped up too much, that he was untrainable. I never had such a miserable Christmas.

Then there was the atomic power station. I came home one holidays to find the place in uproar, the house full of anger and resentment. While I'd been away, word had got out that someone was planning to build an atomic power station just outside the village. The community divided. For, and against. And feelings ran very high.

For – the power station would provide employment. There would be cheaper electricity. It would bring new life to the village.

LET ME TAKE YOU THERE

Against – radioactivity was dangerous, to the land, to the sea, to us. It would be a scar on the landscape. The village would be changed for ever.

At home, the campaign led in part by my mother, we were fervently against the power station. We lost. The plans to build went ahead. So, sometime later, while we were away during another school term, we moved. I came home to another home, which was never home to me. Ripped away again from Bradwell.

I had been young and easy in those days, as Dylan Thomas put it, and was never so young and easy again. It had been my idyll, and it is forever the place of my dreams. I like to revisit my dreams.

I've been back from time to time to Bradwell, written a story or two about it, about the hare, about the power station. In 2018, the whole family went back to celebrate what would have been my mother's hundredth birthday. All of us there, we looked over the wall into the garden of New Hall, walked up past the school, past where the American air force base had been, and went out to St Peter's chapel. We sat for a while, our backs against the sun-warmed stone, each of us deep in our own memories. There were no hares but we did see a skylark rising, singing, descending. And there, in the distance, across the marshes, stood the grey, grim, concrete hulk of the now dysfunctional atomic power station.

On the way back, I came across a bungalow with an interesting name on the gate. New Clear View. And it wasn't in my dreams. Promise. But it will be soon. It's good to laugh as you dream.

PASSING IT ON

2022

The Times *Commission on Education*.

'There is a tide in the affairs of men.'

We have had good cause in recent days to pause, to take stock, to think again. There was a time, in and around the year I was born in, 1943, when the people of this country and others were enduring the devastating trauma of world war. They had partially fended off defeat but were certainly not yet on the road to victory. But they believed in ultimate victory, however remote it must then have seemed. And that gave that generation hope, and with it the determination to create a better, fairer world after the war was over and won, to begin to conceive a new beginning for all the people.

Out of that hope and determination came ideas for radical enabling reform, particularly in the fields of education and health. Their fierce commitment brought about the 1944 Education Act, and in 1947, the National Health Service, and much else besides. The world I grew up in was the product of a generation who recognised how great was the need of the people, and how important were their rights to opportunity and fulfilment, no matter where they lived or their social circumstances. There was a tide turning and they recognised it and responded to it.

My generation has benefited hugely from that turning of the tide, from the inspiration and determination of that generation. We may not have been through a war as they had, but we have lived through the darkest and saddest times we have known, during which we have reflected on so much, from the blackbird singing in the garden to the kindness of a neighbour, to the importance of relationships in our families, to the nature of our society itself. We stopped taking people for granted – indeed, stopped taking life itself for granted.

But we knew the pandemic would be over one day, that the 'normal' we had been so accustomed to was not the normal we wanted to return to, that we should aspire to something better, something fairer, especially for our children. We were witnessing the great benefits and the dedication of the NHS, and indeed its shortcomings.

What of our education system?

For any society, nothing matters more than the children, the seedcorn of its future, the contentment of its people, its future cohesion, its future prosperity, its future place in the world. We know we should have an education system in which the wellbeing of every child is the priority, schools in which learning and creativity go hand in hand, where there is room and expertise for the potential of all children to be recognised and nurtured. We have remarkable teachers all over the country, who are guiding our children intellectually and emotionally through all the complexities of growing up, encouraging them, inspiring them, enriching them, devoting their lives to them. We have thousands of remarkable schools. Yet the system has failed and is failing so many.

At the heart of my concerns, as a teacher one way or another all my life, has been that we have a system of education geared to the system, not the child and the teacher and parent and the school. Life is not a race, not a competition. It is for living, for finding your own voice, your self-worth, your own place in society. It is great teachers, a great school and great parents who help children find themselves, become fully who they are, achieve their aspirations.

It was of course a great honour to sit down, with Rachel Sylvester as chair, with my fellow *Times* Education Commissioners and all the witnesses we called. They came from across our society and spoke, each with deep expertise, knowledge and insight, helping us all to find new ways, explore new ideas in education to help turn the tide for all our children.

I myself come to the table anxious to find, with colleagues, ways to create fairer opportunities for all our children, to break away from a system that creates success, yes, but therefore accepts failure too, to recognise that a good education is the right of every one of us, cradle to grave.

I have my own priorities – we all have round the table. We know that children in this society are still too often denied proper access to libraries and books. Many still leave school barely literate. Yet we know that books are perhaps the greatest and most productive of all pathways to knowledge and understanding and creativity, to widening horizons.

So my priorities. We know how important is our understanding of climate change, its critical effect on us and upon the natural world. For the children of today, this understanding is not just an option but essential to their futures, to all our futures. We know that to understand it, children need to feel connected to that world, that it is theirs to enjoy and to study and to care for. Yet millions, very often those who have least, who are not literate, rarely have the chance to get out there and walk the hills and feel the wind, break the ice on puddles in winter, see a heron rise from a river, dig potatoes, see frogspawn in a pond. It is their world and they have to know they belong to it, that it belongs to all of us, that with that comes responsibility.

So, time to think again, to do better for all our children. There's no greater legacy we can leave them.

Education is for opening eyes and minds and hearts. It is our task to enable all our children to have the educational opportunities to live life to the full, for themselves and for one another, for all of us on this planet.

ALL AROUND THE YEAR

2023

In 1975, Clare and I moved ourselves and the family from Kent, where we had been teaching, to deepest Devon, to Iddesleigh, a small village of thatched cottages and scarcely a hundred souls, with a fourteenth-century perpendicular church, a Methodist chapel and a village hall, then also with a shop with post office and petrol pump. It was and is so remote that if strangers discover it, it is mostly accidental.

There was and is a pub too, the Duke of York. Thatched, log fires and dartboard in winter, a garden and swallows in the summer. Without this pub, we would never have come to Devon all those years ago.

It's a good story, so I shall tell it. It begins in 1949. Clare was seven years old. She had grown up near Hounslow in suburban Middlesex. Her father, Allen Lane, was a great publisher, who had begun Penguin Books in 1935. He knew Iddesleigh because Peggy Rafferty, a dear friend of his from London, with her husband, Sean, now kept the pub in Iddesleigh.

On one of his many visits he brought Clare, his eldest daughter, with him. She loved the place at once, simply put on her wellies and walked. Wherever she walked there were new discoveries: slowworms and lizards in the graveyard, frogspawn and frogs in the ditches, a blackbird singing, swallows nesting and flying, a friendly farmer who let her groom his horse, help with the lambing, gave her lemonade and a sticky bun. She wandered free down the deep lanes, saw flitting goldfinches in the hedgerows and mewing buzzards circling over the fields, found a bluebell wood, followed a stream that ran down to the River Torridge, where Tarka, the otter from Henry Williamson's great masterpiece, had lived. She came back to the pub as evening came on, had tea, went to bed and was up again early next morning and out in her wellies on another voyage of discovery. She had found her paradise.

She came down to spend her holidays with Peggy and Sean at the pub on her own after that, for almost every holiday of her young life. A few years later, we two met, in a scene somewhat reminiscent of Romeo and Juliet. It was on Corfu. She was on a balcony of a bed and breakfast that looked out over a building site, and I was standing there below on a pile of rubble. Anyway . . .

To cut a 60-year story short, it was a brief but turbulent courtship. We were married before we knew it, three children, a dog and a cat or two, several homes and jobs in quick succession, teaching at this school or that, struggling to find our way as we went. Teaching led the way for both of us, our children too. Our lives revolved around children, ours and the schoolchildren we were teaching.

We came to the conclusion that we could only teach so much at school, that both of us had learnt so much more out of school, through our experience of the countryside, by having had the opportunity to spend time close to nature. I had seen in my own childhood and in my teaching just how much children love exploring the world about them.

Clare and I realised how lucky she had been growing up with her walks on the wild side down in Devon; I had had a similar experience in the marshes and fens of the Essex coast near my childhood home in Bradwell on Sea. We knew so many children, especially those in the cities and towns, were missing out on all this, that there was a deep poverty of experience amongst these children. So we decided to do something about it.

Clare's father died all too young in 1970. He left Clare in a position to set up a charity, buy a large house and a small farm so we could invite classes from inner-city schools to come and spend a week a world away, out in the countryside, down on a farm – yes, in Iddesleigh. The idea was not to have them walk around with clipboards and go out on visits to theme parks. No, the children would be the farmers, working with real family farmers who earned their living from the land, so that the children could discover where their food came from, how to look after the animals, grow the vegetables. They would come in all seasons, go out to work in all weathers. From their week on the farm, they would discover that the farm and their work and the animals came first.

All very fine. We had done our research in schools, in university departments of education, taken advice. We would be enriching the lives of these children, extending their knowledge and understanding of their world, giving them a sense of belonging, helping them to see that this countryside was theirs to care for, that nature and wildlife was precious. And perhaps most important, give many children who needed it most a sense of self-worth through the work they would do together as a group with their teachers.

But, as we were to discover, it wasn't fine. We knew, Clare and I, that we would be doing this work alongside the children. Clare knew horses, had reared calves, bottle-fed lambs, and we had kept a few hens, but that was about all. The truth was we had a great deal to learn before we could ever be out there on the farm working with the children who were going to come to us. We could give our charity a name, Farms for City Children, we could buy the house, paint the bunk beds, equip the kitchen, find people to help us in and out of the house, recruit the primary schools to come. But we did not know enough about farming, first hand.

We have had more than our share of luck in this life. It so happened that much of the land around the big old Victorian house we had acquired for the charity – Nethercott House, where the children would live – was already being farmed by the Ward family. One day, by another happy accident, I reversed our Land Rover into a ditch and was unable to drive it out. I was stuck. But then a tractor came along. The driver, who turned out to be David Ward, was one of the farmer's sons. He helped me out of my embarrassment with a cheery and knowing smile.

The same day, we were welcomed into the Ward family, met John and Hettie, and their children Peter, Graham, David and Liz. Soon enough, a few weeks later, we were all sitting down over scones and tea, discussing how we might work together as partners on creating Farms for City Children. Everything fell into place. They would go on farming the land rent free, and in return, they would work, every day during school terms, alongside us, and with the children from the cities.

So that I could be properly prepared, I began working alongside the Ward family, milking cows, feeding sheep and

ALL AROUND THE YEAR

pigs, haymaking, mucking out. I discovered muscles I never knew I had, learnt how hard and unremitting the work was, but how rewarding too.

It was Ted Hughes, a neighbour and good friend by now, who suggested it would be a good idea for me to write a diary of the year, to focus my mind on the rhythm of the farm, on the business and the detail, how the seasons come and go. So I did. Once the year was over, I showed it to him and he said it had to be a book. And he suggested writing a poem for each month. I didn't argue!

Other near neighbours we had got to know well and who had become good friends were James and Robin Ravilious. James' wondrous photographs of pastoral life in Devon were already well known. He had taken many on the Wards' farm, so they knew him. I knew the diary would benefit hugely from his pictures. And Robin, already an accomplished illustrator, would draw some beautiful vignettes.

In the end, the book was a joy to make because it was all done with friends and neighbours, who knew and loved the place. And it served its purpose too, as Ted thought it would. It is the record of my year of apprenticeship. I learnt farming the hard way, and brought all the intensity of that work and the satisfaction too, to our work with the children who came.

FUNNY THING, GETTING OLDER

Farms for City Children goes on still, week after week, year after year – foot and mouth disease and pandemics allowing. Running a charity, like running a farm, is always a struggle. But on we go, with new, younger people running it, with fresh energy and ideas.

Nethercott was the pioneer farm. There are two others now, Treginnis near St David's in Pembrokeshire, and Wick Court near Arlingham in Gloucestershire. The charity is nearly 50 years old. Over 100,000 urban children have now spent a week of their young lives down on the farm with their teachers. They have memories, such memories. And we have too, all of us who work and have worked at Farms for City Children. Looking back over the years, I can honestly say that Farms for City Children is the best story I never wrote, or maybe it's *Wherever My Wellies Take Me,* the book Clare and I wrote together.

THE VOICES OF CHILDREN

2006

A Play

From the BBC radio series The Invention of Childhood *by Hugh Cunningham, presented by Michael Morpurgo.*

It was Beaty Rubens, a wonderful producer at BBC Radio 4, who had the idea of creating a series on childhood through the ages. Hugh Cunningham was asked to write it. I was asked to present it. I came away with a far wider understanding of childhood and education, of how schools were and are for our children.

I became so immersed in the subject that I wrote this play.

—

Present day. The communal gardens in an apartment block in west London.

Centre stage is a great, uprooted oak tree, the massive root system facing the audience. Beneath the roots is a large crater.

FUNNY THING, GETTING OLDER

A children's birthday party is in full swing (the children aged between seven and ten). There's a game of musical chairs going on without the chairs. Some 25 children are there, all in historical costumes of various periods from Anglo-Saxon through medieval to Victorian, except for two: **Hugh**, *aged eight, dressed as Bart Simpson, and his sister* **Beaty**, *dressed as Marge Simpson. Both are wearing easily identifiable cut-out cardboard hairpieces. They are dancing in a circle with the others (***Hugh*** obviously unwilling) to the strains of Boney M. The mood is wild. The music stops. Last to sit down is* **Hugh** *because he isn't paying attention.*

Children (cry out in unison) 'Hugh! Hugh!'

Hugh *is out. He stomps off, fed up. The dancing circle continues with the music and then unravels, leaving* **Hugh** *alone with the tree. He sits down on the edge of the crater, disconsolate, chucking stones at the roots. We hear the music stop again.* **Beaty** *joins him, really fed up.*

Hugh I wasn't trying anyway.
Beaty Nor me.
Hugh *(still chucking stones)* I could kill her.
Beaty Who?

THE VOICES OF CHILDREN

Hugh Mum. I told her, didn't I? Historical. The costumes for the party had to be historical. But she always knows best, doesn't she?

Beaty Tell me about it.

Hugh *(Mimicking his mother sarcastically.)* 'Oh, no, Hugh, I talked to Jamie's grandma about it, and she definitely said hysterical not historical. And hysterical, dear, means funny, if you didn't know. And Bart Simpson's funny – you're always telling me.' And then she goes and makes me wear this . . . thing. *(He whips off his hairpiece and hurls it into the crater, and* **Beaty** *does the same in solidarity.)* I'll kill her.

Beaty You're not allowed.

Hugh And that's another thing. Why should she tell me what to wear anyway? They're always making the rules. Dad's just as bad. It's all they do, sit around making rules and drinking cups of coffee.

Beaty We've got to have rules. It's like the days of the week. Monday and Tuesday and that. You wouldn't know when to go to school, else. They are sort of like birthdays. You can't grow older unless you have birthdays, can you?

Hugh Who wants to be old anyway? You get all wrinkly and you get hairs in your ears like Grandpa. No, thank you! You know what I want? I want to stay eight years old for ever and make up my own rules. And the first rule will be that I make the rules.

Beaty *(Not listening. She is looking at the fallen oak tree.)* It's sad.

Hugh What is?

Beaty That tree. It got old, didn't it? I really loved it. It was the oldest in London, Mum said. Been here for ever.

Hugh Couldn't have been for ever. Nothing's for ever, is it? *(He's gazing at the upturned roots.)* There's hundreds and hundreds of roots. Which was the first, I wonder?

Beaty And who planted it?

Enter silently, and without them noticing, a sturdy-looking 11-year-old Anglo-Saxon boy, **Cedd.** *He is scantily clad in furs.* **Cedd** *will serve as the narrator throughout the play, donning different period costumes on stage as the centuries pass.*

Cedd I did. I planted it. *(He bends down and picks up an acorn.)* With this. Then when I died they buried me beside it because it was my tree. *(He scoops up a* *handful of earth and lets it pour through his fingers.)* Not a lot of me left, is there?

Hugh *(Terrified, like his sister, at the implication of what has just been said. They have backed away,* **Hugh** *hiding behind* **Beaty** *for protection.)* Who's he?

Beaty *(Whispering.)* He wasn't at the party?

Hugh Is he a ghost or what?

Beaty Think so, and he hasn't got much clothes on either. Looks like Stig of the Dump.

Cedd You should plant another one.

Beaty Why us?

Cedd Because it was my tree and you are my descendants, my relations. You came from me, just like this tree came from an acorn. *(To* **Beaty**.*)* You could plant it together. *(To* **Hugh**.*)* And you could put the acorn in, dig the hole for it too. I always had to do the digging when I was your age. They always give us boys the dirty jobs, don't they?

Hugh *(Less fearful now, glad of the proffered solidarity.)* Huh, tell me about it.

Cedd All right, I will. You'd better sit down though, because it's quite a story.

FUNNY THING, GETTING OLDER

Beaty and Hugh are nonplussed by this response, but they sit on the edge of the crater. Just as they do so, onto the stage come all the 'party' children, ghosts now, every one of them, and moving slowly. **Beaty** *and* **Hugh** *are alarmed. They can see the transition and know what it means.*

It's my story, and your story and their story too. They were there. They'll tell you all about it. They'll tell it as they found it, as they saw it, as it happened. And they are all your ancestors, like me. But it's the story of all the children who have known this land and breathed this air. It begins with me. I was digging a grave. My own little sister's grave. She was called Hedda.

From the chorus comes a diminutive Anglo-Saxon girl, Hedda, very frail and pale. As with all the children from the chorus who come forward, she speaks directly to the audience.

Hedda I am full yong
I was born yesterday.
Death is ful hasty
On me to been wreke.

THE VOICES OF CHILDREN

Hedda *rejoins the chorus.*

Cedd *(Wearing a medieval costume now.)* More than anything it was hunger and cold that took us young, took us from our families, took us from this world. Every mother, every father, every sister, every brother knew the pity of it. It went on like this for hundreds of years, a massacre of the innocents. We had a day of our very own, a day to remember how King Herod had killed all the innocent children, but it was a day when we remembered all the children. Childermas it was called, 28 December every year, one day when we could be just who we wanted to be. It was a day when we could say what we liked, a day a boy could be a bishop, and even give a sermon, like John did in Gloucester Cathedral in front of hundreds of people. He told them.

John, *escorted by two other children, comes forward from the chorus. He's in tattered clothes. His escorts dress him up like a bishop, and give him a bishop's mitre and crook. The mitre is too big and slips down over his face. They try again to put it on but it won't stay up. So they hold it up for him as he gives his sermon. He does*

FUNNY THING, GETTING OLDER

this with bishop-like pomposity, but he means every word.

John Young babes and little children are simple, without gyle, innocent, without harme and all pure without corruption. You shall perceive in them no manner of malice, no envy, no disdayne, no hurtfulness, no synfull affection, no pride, no ambition, no singularities, no desire of honour, of riches, of carnality, of revenging, of quitting evil for evil.

Children *sing 'The Coventry Carol'.*

Cedd The trouble was, once the day was over, we were treated just the same as we had been before, worked to the bone, beaten whenever they felt like it. But once out of sight, we could be children again. We could wander where we wanted, do what we pleased, play blind man's bluff and hide and seek – and football too.
Hugh Football?
Cedd They made it out of a pig's bladder.
Cedd Girls didn't play football. They didn't have nearly so much fun as boys did.

THE VOICES OF CHILDREN

Beaty Tell me about it!

Cedd *(Not understanding this phrase.)* Abigail knows all about it, don't you Abigail? She was made to learn this and recite it often, so she'd be a good girl, weren't you, Abigail?

Abigail *comes forward demurely.*

Abigail *(Speaking very properly.)*
In temperate and patient innocence
With modesty of bearing and of dress
And showed in speech a modesty no less
She used no fancy term in affectation
Of learning, but according to her station
She spoke in all and everything she said
She showed she was good and gently bred.

Cedd And did you show you were good and gently bred?

Abigail *(Screaming with frustration and rage and stamping her foot.)* No! No! No! *(She runs off the stage.)*

Beaty Good for you.

Cedd But there were rules for boys and girls alike. Then, as if there weren't enough rules already, someone went and invented school. No one wanted to go. I mean, why did they do that?

FUNNY THING, GETTING OLDER

Hugh Dunno. I think they are still trying to work that out.

Michael *comes forward looking doleful, rubbing his backside.*

Michael My master looketh as he were mad
'Where has thou been, thou sorry lad?'
'Milking ducks, as my mother bade.'
It was no marvel that I were sad
My master peppered my tail with good speed
He would not leave till it did bleed
Much sorrow have he for his deed.
I would my master were a hare
And all his books greyhounds were
And I myself a jolly hunter
To blow my horn I would not spare
For if he were dead I would not care!
Beaty *(Aside to* **Hugh**.*)* They speak funny, don't they?
Hugh That's cos they always spoke in poetry in those days. He's getting changed again. Looks like a Tudor now. I done the Tudors in school – the Armada and that.

THE VOICES OF CHILDREN

Cedd *(Changed into Elizabethan costume.)* I've always liked stories. Bible stories, saints' stories, Robin Hood – if anyone should have been a saint, it was him, helping the poor like he did. But riddles were my favourite. Here, can you work this one out? Ready?

Beaty and **Hugh** *(together)* Ready!

Cedd Two legs sat upon three legs
With one leg in his lap.
In comes four legs
And runs away with one leg.
Up jumps two legs,
Throws it after four legs
And makes him bring back one leg.

*(**Beaty** and **Hugh** are stumped.)*

You do go to school, do you? *(They nod.)* Well, they didn't teach you then, did they? Watch this.

Riddle is now acted out by the children. **Simon** *comes on with a three-legged stool, sits on it. He has a leg of mutton in his lap. Dog comes in (***Abigail** *on four legs), snatches leg of mutton and runs off stage.* **Simon** *throws stool off stage at dog who comes back on, tail between* *legs, and brings back bone, licked clean. Dog tries to look happy and contrite at the same time.*

Cedd See? Good, eh?

Beaty Were they really all our relations?

Cedd Every one of them, including the dog. *(Suddenly serious.)* They couldn't all play silly games, though. Lots of our relatives never lived to grow up. Nehemiah, she died when she was very little. *(Nehemiah comes on – in nightclothes, supported by her father.)* These were the last words she ever spoke.

Nehemiah Father, I go abroad tomorrow and bring you a plum pie. *(As she leaves him reluctantly, she lets go his hand.)*

Father Such a child I never saw, for such a child I bless God. Thou gavest her to us, thou hast taken her from us, blessed be the name of the Lord.

Cedd *(Shrugging on another costume, that of a boy of the Civil War, with a sword at his side.)* What do you think? *(He gives a twirl.)*

Beaty Cool.

Hugh When are we now?

Cedd Just after the Civil War, after they'd chopped off Charles I's head. The Royalists wore better clothes, but the Puritans won, and, unfortunately, they were very keen on schools. So even more of us had to go to school now. *(William comes on, a boy, a Puritan.)* But William was a farm boy, so he got lucky sometimes.

William From the age of 10 or 12 years, we were very much better off in the schoole, espetialy in the spring and summer season, plow time, turfe time, hay time and harvest, looking after the sheep, helping at plough, making hay and shearing two of us at 13 or 14 years old being equal to one man shearer, so we made small progress in Latin, for what we got in winter we forgot in summer. We got what writing we had in winter. *(Sees schoolmaster coming.)* Look out. Here's the master. I'm off.

Alexander, *dressed as a schoolmaster, hurries on, shaking his cane in fury after William. Suddenly seeing the audience, he remembers the dignity of his position. He mimics a teacher.*

Alexander Obedience is one of the capital benefits arising from a public education, to break the ferocity of human nature, to subdue the passions and to impress

FUNNY THING, GETTING OLDER

the principles of religion and morality – this is the first object to be attended to by all schoolmasters who know their duty. William! *(He goes off stage.)* William! Come back this minute, you rascal, you!

Cedd *(In eighteenth-century coat and hat now.)* But to be honest, those children who were in school were the lucky ones – despite schoolmasters like him. You won't want to see this but you have to. It's part of the story.

A poor mother comes on, carrying a baby in her arms. She looks around and puts the baby down, kisses it, then runs off, weeping.

Many children were very poor, and poor meant hungry. Another mouth to feed was a mouth too many. Some were left in church porches. Worse still, some became beggars and a few even ended up as slaves. Slaves! Can you believe it?

Two street children come on, **William** *and* **Joan**. *One crouches to pick up the baby.*

Hugh Who are they?
Cedd Children who never lived to laugh and play. Listen.

THE VOICES OF CHILDREN

William Is this a holy thing to see
   In a rich and fruitful land
   Babes reduced to misery
   Fed with cold and usurious hand?
Joan Is that trembling cry a song?
   Can it be a song of joy?
   And so many children poor
   It is a land of poverty.

William *and* **Joan** *(together)*
   And their sun does never shine
   And their fields are bleak and bare
   And their ways are filled with thorns
   It is eternal winter there.
Beaty They make me feel so sad. Are they our relations too?
Cedd We all are.
Hugh Were we always poor?
Cedd No, but even if you weren't poor, children could have a hard time of it. Rules again. Rules, rules. Elizabeth was your great-great-grandmother – doesn't look like it, does she?

Elizabeth *comes forward, middle class, in her early teens, confident.*

FUNNY THING, GETTING OLDER

Elizabeth The milk rebellion was crushed immediately. In his dressing gown, with his whip in his hand, Father attended our breakfast . . . That disgusting milk! He began with me: my beseeching look was answered by a sharp cut, followed by as many more as were necessary to empty the basin. And bathtime was worse still. A large tub stood in the kitchen court, the ice on top of which had often to be broken before our horrid plunge into it. We were brought down from the very top of the house, four pairs of stairs, with only a cotton cloak over our night-gowns, just to chill us completely before the dreadful shock. How I screamed, begged, prayed, entreated to be saved. Half the tender-hearted maids in tears besides me. All to no use. Millar, our nurse, had her orders.

Cedd But once she got outside away from her father, away from the rules . . .

There follows a game of 'drop handkerchief'. Children, including **Elizabeth**, *alternating girl/boy circle around in a ring. Elizabeth drops the handkerchief behind* **Piers'** *back. She runs off.* **Piers** *picks it up and is held by the girls on the other side so* **Elizabeth** *can get away. He breaks free finally. She rejoins the*

THE VOICES OF CHILDREN

ring, just as he catches her. They go to the centre of the ring and kiss.

The children, in nine couples, now come forward and recite a couplet each, before the next couple take their place.

First couple The Sun does arise
   And make happy the skies
Second couple The merry bells ring
   To welcome the spring
Third couple The skylark and thrush
   The birds of the bush
Fourth couple Sing louder around
   To the bells' cheerful sound
Fifth couple While our sports shall be seen
   On the echoing Green
Sixth couple Old John with white hair
   Does laugh away care
Seventh couple Sitting under the oak
   Among the old folk
Eighth couple They laugh at our play
   And soon they all say
Ninth couple 'Such were the joys
   When we all, girls and boys

FUNNY THING, GETTING OLDER

Children *(all together)*
In our youth time were seen
'On the Echoing Green.'

Beaty Were they Victorians? We've done Victorians in class. *Oliver Twist* and all that stuff.

Cedd *(Donning a Victorian hat and coat.)* We're coming to them now. And you won't like what you are going to hear. There never was a worse time than this for children. Children should be seen and not heard. That's how they were treated up at the big houses. And that was bad enough. (**George** *comes on carrying his sweep's brushes over each shoulder, blackened, coughing, exhausted.*) For the poor children, the working children, it was a lot worse. This is George. He died when he was 11.

George I was a climbing boy, I was. I was apprentice to a master sweep. In Cambridge, it was. The last chimney I did was at Fulbourne Hospital. I didn't want to go up again. I was bad in my chest, see. But they made me. They pricked the soles of my feet to make me go up. They set straw alight under me. I had to go up, didn't I? When I died, they opened me up and they found all my lungs and my windpipe was full of black powder. I suffocated to death. Couldn't breathe. It was good to die. Didn't suffer no more after that.

Cedd There were thousands of climbing boys like George. Wherever they wanted cheap labour they used children – in the factories and the mills, down the mines, in the dirt and the dark, like Sarah – oh yes, girls too went down the mines.

Six children come in pushing a coal cart, all bent to their work, all blackened, all barely able to keep going. They stop and lean on the cart. One of them, **Sarah**, *straightens herself slowly.*

Sarah I work in the Gauber pit. I have to work without a light and I'm scared. Sometimes I sing when I've a light, but not in the dark. I dare not sing then. I don't like being in the pit. I'm very sleepy when I go sometimes in the morning. I go to Sunday school and read *Reading Made Easy*. I would like to be at school far better than in the pit.

Cedd Do you know the saddest story I ever heard? It was about a factory girl who had to get up early every morning to go to work. One morning, she was sick, too weak to get up. She was lying in her father's arms.

FUNNY THING, GETTING OLDER

She woke up and the first thing she thought was that it must be time to go to work. 'Father, is it time?' she said. 'Father, is it time?' Then she sank back in his arms and died.

The sound of a drum and marching feet. A protest march of ragged factory children, carrying banners reading: 'Father, is it time?', 'Behold and Weep!'

Factory children *(shouting)* No more! No more!

Suddenly, the children are still and silent. A single child, **Clare***, steps forward.*

Clare The young lambs are bleating in the meadows,
 The young birds are chirping in the nest,
 The young fauns are playing with the shadows,
 The young flowers are blowing towards the West.
 But the young, young children, O my brothers,
 They are weeping bitterly!
 They are weeping in the playtime of the others,
 In the country of the free.

THE VOICES OF CHILDREN

Children pick up the echo of the last word and chant it in time with the drumbeat of the protest march, punching the air as they go off.

Children *(chanting)* Free! Free! Free! Free! Free!

Hugh *and* **Beaty**, *deeply upset and angry, jump up and join in the chanting as the children leave.*

Cedd There's more. (**Hugh** *and* **Beaty** *sit down again.*) There were the street children like Jim. It was a cold winter's night and it was late. Look.

Enter **Jim**, *in rags, from stage left. He sits down hugging his knees, shivering.* **Dr Barnardo** *(a child dressed up) comes from stage right. He notices* **Jim** *and goes over to him.*

Dr Barnardo Come, my lad, had you better not get home? It's very late. Mother will be coming for you.
Jim Please, sir, let me stop.
Dr Barnardo Why do you want to stay?
Jim Please, sir, do let me stay. I won't do no harm.
Dr Barnardo Your mother will wonder what kept you so late.

FUNNY THING, GETTING OLDER

Jim I ain't got no mother.

Dr Barnardo Haven't got a mother, boy? Where do you live?

Jim Don't live nowhere.

Dr Barnardo Do you mean to say, my boy, that you have no home, that you have no mother or father?

Jim That's the truth on't, sir. I ain't telling you no lie about it.

Dr Barnardo But where did you sleep last night?

Jim Down Whitechapel, sir, in one of them cars as is filled with 'ay. I won't do 'arm, sir, if you let me stay.

Dr Barnardo Are there other children sleeping out like you?

Jim Oh yes, lots. 'eaps on 'em, sir. More'n I could count.

Dr Barnardo You come along with me, lad. I'll find you somewhere warm, somewhere you can stay, and a good hot meal, too.

Jim Honest?

Dr Barnardo Honest. *(He helps Jim up and they leave.)*

Cedd That was Dr Barnardo. He looked after thousands of street children just like Jim.

Beaty So there were some good people?

Cedd Lots of them, luckily for you. If there hadn't been, like as not you'd be living on the streets or working in factories still. Things got better all right. But not in a hurry. Look at your great-grandfather now. James he was called. He was 13. First day at work.

James *comes on, sees the audience, and stops to tell them. He's very pleased with himself, dressed in his new working clothes.*

James Said goodbye to my schooling at Spotland Board School. Off to work at Heaps. Fifty-five and a half hour working week for 10 shillings and sixpence, a fortune for Mother. Mother rigged me out in this at a total cost of 15 shillings. Not bad, eh? *(Does a turn.)* Corduroy trousers, leather braces. Brown cap. Got a button on top and the scarf to keep the wind out. Proper little man, Mother called me. And she's right. I'm a breadwinner now and proud of it. Got to go. Mustn't be late on your first day. *(Lifts his cap and runs off.)*
Beaty *(Gazing after him.)* Dreamy. Looks like Leonardo DiCaprio in that ship film, you know, *Titanic*.
Hugh Looks a lot like me, I reckon.
Beaty *(scoffing)* You!

FUNNY THING, GETTING OLDER

Hugh Well, he is my great-grandfather.
Beaty He's mine too.
Cedd *(Pulls on a jacket and flat cap like James's.)* He married your great-grandmother young, very young. They had a baby. He went off to fight in the First World War. Never came back. Nearly a million of them never came back. That was the First World War.

Children come on stage, dancing. They chant raucously, as in street singing, as they dance.

Children When the war is over and the Kaiser's dead
He's no gaun' tae Heaven wi' the eagle on his head.
For the Lord says 'No! He'll have tae go below
For all he's dressed up and nowhere tae go.'
Cedd Then a few years later they had a Second World War.

Children begin doing a conga around the stage.

Children *(Singing – same tune as before.)*
When the war is over Hitler will be dead
He hopes to go to heaven with a crown upon his head.

THE VOICES OF CHILDREN

But the Lord says 'No! You'll have to go below,
There's only room for Churchill, so cheery-cheery
oh!'

Sounds of siren going off and bombs falling.

Beaty I thought you said things got better for kids.
Cedd They did.
Beaty There's nothing better about wars, is there? How can wars ever be better?
Cedd No, but sometimes wars can make people stop and think a bit. Only good thing about them. They know they have to try to make things better for their grandchildren, look after them better, feed them better.

*A girl, **Charis**, in pigtails, comes on hopscotching along the pavement on her way back home from school, talking to herself.*

Charis I hate school dinners. I hate school dinners.
 (chanting) Splishy splashy custard
 Dead dog's eyes
 All mixed up with giblet pies.

FUNNY THING, GETTING OLDER

Spread it on the butty nice and thick
Swallow it down with a bucket of sick.

From behind, the children echo her chant. **Charis** *stops her hopscotching, spooked by the echo. She runs off.*

Hugh Who was that?
Cedd *(In modern clothes now, baseball cap, Chelsea shirt etc.)* Your mum.
Hugh and **Beaty** *(together)* Our mum!
Cedd Yep. And then after her there was you and you, and after you . . . that's how it happens, how things keep going. That's why you've got to plant that acorn I gave you. It's what we're here for, to keep things going, make new life, and make things better if we can.
Beaty Yes, and we will too.
Hugh *(Kneeling down.)* Here? Do I plant it here?
Cedd Where you like.

Hugh *hands the acorn to* **Beaty** *and digs with his hands on the edge of the crater. As he does so, the chorus of children from the ages emerges to form a semicircle around them.* **Hugh** *and* **Beaty** *do not*

THE VOICES OF CHILDREN

notice. **Beaty** *kneels now to plant the acorn, and they both fill in the hole, stand up and look down as if waiting for the tree to grow.* **Hugh** *nudges* **Beaty**. *The semicircle has become a circle. He has noticed they are now surrounded by all the children. They feel a little threatened until* **Cedd**, *with them in the centre of the circle, reassures them.*

Cedd They've come to say goodbye. We all have. But first they wanted to play a game with you. It's a game they know and you'll know. A game all children have always known. Blind man's bluff.

Hugh Can I ask you something? Why the shirt? Why Chelsea?

Cedd They're champions again, aren't they?

Hugh How come you know so much?

Cedd I don't know who's going to win next year, do I?

Hugh I do. Manchester United.

Cedd You up for blind man's bluff? *(He holds out the blindfolds.)*

Hugh Both of us at once?

Cedd Why not? We can change the rules if we want to, can't we?

FUNNY THING, GETTING OLDER

Cedd *ties the blindfolds on both* **Hugh** *and* **Beaty**. *He turns them round and round. They begin to grope forwards, arms, outstretched, finding each other first. The children in the circle laugh, loving the fun of it. The circle of historical children, hands joined, begins to turn. We hear the distant strains of Boney M. They move to the rhythm of it in a flowing dance, in time-synchronised steps.* **Cedd** *joins the circle and, after a while, leads the children off, leaving* **Hugh** *and* **Beaty** *groping alone onstage.*

The music is louder now as the children return, in the same costumes but as the party children, dancing excitedly, hysterically (hands not joined), as they form the dancing circle again. **Cedd** *is not amongst them.* **Beaty** *catches one of the children and rips off her blindfold.* **Hugh** *does the same. They turn around and around, wondering, wondering. The circle turns into disco dancing.* **Hugh** *and* **Beaty** *walk through the dancers to the front of the stage, still wondering about all they've seen. The music dies away, the party children dance on – in silence now. From amongst them, from the crater, a young tree slowly rises. (A child as a tree.) The children see it, stop dancing and watch in wonder.* **Hugh** *and*

THE VOICES OF CHILDREN

Beaty *turn and see it too. The two join hands, backs to the audience. The children all back away, offstage, reverently, leaving the stage to the tree and* **Hugh** *and* **Beaty**. *Then they too leave the stage slowly. The tree stands alone.*

The End.

LITTLE AMAL

2021

This piece was inspired by the 3.5-metre-high puppet created at Good Chance Theatre by Handspring Puppets, who made War Horse. Little Amal has travelled the globe widely since 2015, raising awareness of the plight of refugees all over the world.

As I write this, in the safety and comfort of our cottage in Devon, many thousands of refugees from Afghanistan, and from Syria and elsewhere, in fear of their lives, are desperate to flee their country, to find safety, to find a home where guns and bombs and hate and fear do not rule. Many are hoping to find a new life here, amongst us. Our country is their Shangri La.

I happen to know of one refugee child, a 12-year-old girl from Syria, called Little Amal. She is making her way north, up through the mountains of Greece, at the start of an epic journey of some 8,000 kilometres. She is following in the footsteps of millions like her, all seeking refuge from war and hunger, persecution and poverty, longing for a home, a roof over her head, a school, a future, work and the warmth of a welcome. Like so many of the estimated 60 million refugees now on the move throughout the world, Little Amal is a child alone. But in a way, she is not a child, and she is not alone.

I will explain. I have never met Little Amal. I feel I know her. But I don't. I know of many like her. We all do. We have seen on our screens a child rescued from the ruins of a bombed-out house, in some nameless town, now reduced to rubble; refugee children trudging the roads, huddled against the cold. We have seen a child carried up out of the sea, lifeless; another lying on the shore, lifeless. We've heard of the extraordinary kindness of so many people here who have offered their spare room, clothes, food, whatever they can, to the new refugees from Afghanistan.

But we've also been hearing about measures to prevent them from landing at all, to turn them away, to force them to go elsewhere; measures to deal with 'the refugee problem'. To witness daily so much suffering, week after week, year after year, is hard to bear. We switch off, look the other way. I looked the other way for a long time when I should have known better. Global Britain has been doing this too. We all should have known better. Historically, many millions of us here come from families who first arrived in this country as refugees, as migrants. We are in large part a nation of refugees, of migrants. Maybe because of this we have had a long and honourable tradition over the centuries of welcoming in strangers in need. Over the centuries, they have brought with them their ancient cultures, their traditions, their talents, and have enriched us immeasurably. They are what makes Britain genuinely global.

Little Amal is coming to us. Right now, she is on her way. Full of determination and hope. She has nothing else. To reach us, she must put one foot in front of the other, for months on end, enduring the pain, the cold, the heat, the hunger and the hostility. Every smile, every helping hand will keep her going. Of course, who we welcome in, how many can come and stay, these are immensely difficult and sensitive questions. That's for sure. Some say we've taken in enough already, that there is no room for more. But surely, just as we now fully acknowledge our global responsibility to restore the world about us, the world we ourselves have damaged, so we must play our part, as one of the richest nations on earth, to welcome in as many refugees as we can, to give them safe haven with us, to treat them right, as we know we should.

Sometimes we have not treated them right. I went once to visit The Jungle outside Calais, that cauldron of misery and squalor, a makeshift camp where refugees from the many troubled and needy corners of the world gathered to make the final perilous leap across the Channel to the safety of our shores.

In The Jungle, I met young refugees for the first time, face to face, looking them in the eye. I found myself sitting inside a patchwork plastic tent, talking to them – a dozen or more Afghan boys – exchanging stories and songs. We made friends. I could no longer switch them off, nor look the other way. I felt an overwhelming sense of solidarity with them. I was willing them over the Channel, willing them to be with family again, willing them to find the haven they had travelled so far and endured so much to find.

And I found other friends in that Jungle. I found some remarkable young people from the Good Chance theatre company. They had set up a kind of circus tent where the children of the camp gathered to make and perform their plays, to sing their songs, to tell and listen to stories. Here was an escape for them, from the boredom, the filth, the tension, the loss and tragedy they had all lived through. Here were young people from my country who had recognised there was a need they could help to fulfil. I went home inspired, chastened, thinking. And soon I was thinking: *I can write books about the lives of these refugees, from Iraq, from Afghanistan. That's something I could do. It might not change the world. But it would be something.*

Then Antonia Cohen, a friend of ours, came up with something more constructive, a really purposeful idea. Working with young asylum seekers cooped up in small rooms, lonely and often depressed, she discovered there was something they were all longing to do. Cricket. They wanted to play cricket. Antonia suggested they come down to Devon on a cricket tour. That's what happened. They came, they saw, they conquered! On a sheep field just below our village of Iddesleigh in deepest Devon, a cricket pitch was prepared, of sorts. Well, the Afghan boys won a famous victory. At tea, one of them, gazing out towards the distant hills of Dartmoor, said to me, with tears in his eyes, 'It's like my home in Afghanistan.' They went on to play four other matches. The boys were always courteous and kind, but when it came to the cricket, they showed no mercy. They won every match. They will not forget it, and we will not forget them. Such memories drive away despair.

I don't know if Little Amal plays cricket. I'll ask her when I meet her. Time to tell you about her. You remember Good Chance? Well, it was the idea of this theatre company, after the huge success of their play, *Jungle*, to create a unique travelling drama. They decided to make a 3.5-metre-high puppet of a girl refugee from Syria, and they called her Little Amal. The drama they would play out would be Little Amal's 8,000

LITTLE AMAL

kilometre walk from the refugee camp in Turkey to Manchester. There would be three alternating teams of puppeteers, and they would walk in rain or shine, uphill and down, through villages and towns and cities, all the way up through Europe.

And that's what they're doing . . . this marvel, one step in front of the other, reminding everyone who sees her that she is not 'a problem', but a child longing to find her mother, a child seeking a home where she can be happy, live in peace and make a contribution. Little Amal, like all refugee children heading our way, will go to school with our children, learn and play with them, grow up with them, become one of them, one of us. I shall be there, like many others, like you maybe, to welcome Little Amal as she makes her way from the orchards of Kent, up through the streets of London, to Manchester. I'll be there to hold her hand. Or will she be holding mine? And I shall be writing the story of her great journey, if she will let me. I, for one, will never look the other way again.

SET OUR CHILDREN FREE

2011

I was asked to give the Richard Dimbleby lecture in 2011. The seeds of the conflict today, in 2024, with all its horror and cruelties, were sown long before I went to Gaza, long before this lecture. We do reap what we sow.

A few years ago, I was involved in the making of a documentary for BBC radio called *The Invention of Childhood*. Working on the series gave me a powerful sense of how childhood has evolved over the ages, and how long it took for the lives of children to emerge from the dark ages of poverty, neglect and exploitation.

I discovered also how it is only comparatively recently that we have begun to talk of the rights of children. Thomas Paine's *Rights of Man* was published in 1791. Mary Wollstonecraft's *A Vindication of the Rights of Woman* came out, in response, in 1792. But it wasn't until the twentieth century that children's rights began to be taken seriously, culminating in 1989, with the introduction of the United Nations Convention on the Rights of the Child. The convention declares that every child should have a right to a name and to a nationality, access to healthcare, to play and recreation, to survival, to liberty and to an education. Who could possibly object to that? Well, you'd be surprised.

It is yet to be ratified by two countries at the United Nations – Somalia and the United States. We in Britain have ratified the convention but, I wonder, do we live by it? How is it that so many children in this country, and the world over, still never know the joys of childhood? Here, I will confine myself to three primary rights as laid down in the UN Convention, rights that all children should enjoy: the right to survival, to liberty and to education. It will be a personal and sometimes uncomfortable journey. We shall discover that even under our own noses these rights have been and still are woefully neglected. For the most part, I'm going to use my own experience as a guide. I've been a parent, a grandparent, a teacher in one way or another for 35 years, and a writer for children. So children have long been at the centre of my world.

Less is more when it comes to statistics. A few will do. It is estimated that today, 8 million children a year die before the age of five. That's a holocaust of children every year. Sixty-nine million children never go to school. A billion of the world's children still live in poverty. But let us not imagine for one moment that it is only elsewhere in the world that the rights of children are so conspicuously neglected. In our own country, 3.5 million children are still mired in poverty. And some of the most vulnerable of these have been appallingly treated.

Two lines from William Blake:
A robin redbreast in a cage
Puts all Heaven in a rage.

Over two hundred years ago, Blake, that great visionary poet, pricked the conscience of a nation to consider the plight of its children. I spoke those same two lines to camera a year or so ago, outside the barbed wire fence of a place called Yarl's Wood in Bedfordshire, an immigration removal centre for asylum seekers, including families and children, a kind of holding pen before deportation. Yarl's Wood was opened in November 2001. Since then, thousands of asylum-seeking families and children had been effectively imprisoned there, sometimes for months. I was with a BBC film crew for *The Politics Show*. We wanted to go in but it was not permitted. I am not surprised, for something deeply shameful to us all was going on inside that place.

Until 2008, I'd never heard of Yarl's Wood – very few people had, we like to keep quiet about such things – until I happened to see a play, called *Motherland* by Natasha Walter, a play later staged at the House of Commons. It was put on to raise awareness of the plight of these asylum seekers and the injustice being done to them. The play was largely told through the eyes of the children imprisoned there – their own stories, in their own words. I watched the play in disbelief. This was happening in my country, in Britain, where we so value childhood, where – supposedly – we so cherish children.

In the play, we hear the story of Meltem, a 13-year-old girl from Turkey. These are her own words:

My name is Meltem. It was 7 o'clock in the morning in August. At our home in Doncaster. We've lived there for six years. They banged and banged on the door. As soon as my mum opened the door they rushed in. There were twelve of them, twelve big men. They took us to the police station. They told us to wait, they said there is a car coming to take you to the removal centre.

The car came and it was awful. It had a cage. For a minute I thought to myself, am I an animal? The journey took a long time and this is where we ended up, here in Yarl's Wood. I tell you it has no difference from a jail.

It has been more than two months I'm here so far. For education in here, I get maths for nine-year-olds and jigsaw puzzles. No. They don't give you an education here. I don't think you can get educated when you know you're in a prison. I saw an officer slapping a little two-year-old baby because he was playing with lights. And I saw a mother crying for her baby because they wouldn't take her to healthcare. The officers were being really nasty, like they are just lowering people down and saying words to make them sadder. At school, I was good at science, maths, and history. I wanted to become a doctor. My teachers, they were really kind. I miss them all so much, just being at school and doing normal things, with my friends.[1]

So for a decade or more, we had been locking up asylum-seeking children, like Meltem, in this country, thousands of them, and all of them innocent of any crime. But Meltem's story doesn't end here. She finished up, after an attempted deportation, in Bedford hospital. Sir Al Aynsley-Green was the enlightened children's commissioner at the time. He visited her in hospital. He'd been a children's doctor himself for 30 years. These are his words:

I talked to this vulnerable child about her experiences. I felt that this case exposed such glaring faults in the treatment of child asylum seekers that I should express my concerns to the Home Office. Since then, my office has been deluged by appeals from supporters of other children in detention. I cannot take up individual cases. But this begs the issue, who, in the present system, does have the power to take up their cases and defend their rights? I hope you understand the enormity of my fury. To see this young child, who is not much older than my own granddaughter; one cannot help thinking, what would one want for one's own children in that situation? The impact on the children themselves of such treatment is profound, not least because they are also witnessing the enormous distress of their parents. In many of the practices we see in our asylum system, there is an absence of common decency, humanity and dignity. One has to struggle not to be too emotional.[2]

This story, at least, has an ending we might call happy. Meltem and her mother were released and now, after years of protest by a dedicated group of campaigners, the government has changed its mind. Although Yarl's Wood itself has not been closed, at least no children are locked up in there any more. But we have to ask how on earth men and women, many of them no doubt parents themselves, sat around a table and thought this was an acceptable idea in the first place? It was done, of course, out of pragmatism and political expediency, the interests of the child quite ignored. This was no petty case of right or wrong, but a flagrant abuse of rights. A great wrong has, in part at least, been redressed. But had it not been for the determination of these valiant campaigners I fear nothing would have changed.

Fired up by their example and by the sufferings of the children concerned, I wrote my own story, a fictional tale, of a young Afghan boy who, along with his mother and a stray dog called Shadow, escapes from Afghanistan. They make their way to England only to find themselves, six years later, locked up in Yarl's Wood. Writing the story was my way, I suppose, of dealing with the feelings I had about such a grave injustice.

One day, we will apologise for Yarl's Wood, just as we did over those children forcibly expatriated to Australia after the Second World War – another example of what might be called 'the bureaucracy of neglect' – not intentional maybe, but cruel all the same in its collateral damage.

It may seem that I seek out causes to write about. It doesn't happen that way. Rather, they seem to seek me out and very often it is children themselves who bring them to my attention. I was in Jordan, in Amman, with Clare some ten years ago, and had the opportunity of talking about stories to Jordanian children – about 80 per cent of whom are Palestinian refugees, many of them still living in camps. At the end of one session, I asked the teenagers whether they had any questions. To start with, they were not forthcoming. But once the first found the courage to speak, the floodgates opened and I was bombarded with questions – mixed metaphor I know, but I like mixed metaphors. It's probably why I got a third-class degree, but I'm sure it was a good third!

Anyway, the question-and-answer session became very relaxed and jolly. Then I was taken completely by surprise. A teenage girl who had said nothing up to now got to her feet. 'I don't want to ask a question,' she began, 'I want to tell you something.' The room went quiet.

'You say you write stories that are always based on what is real and true, something you feel strongly about. I want to tell you something real and true. My family lives here in Jordan, but I do not belong here. I belong in Palestine. It is my home but I can't live there because it is occupied. I can't even go there. I want you to tell a story about us.'

I said, 'I don't know enough about the lives of Palestinians, nor about the conflict in the Middle East, certainly not enough to write a story about it.'

'But you could find out, couldn't you?' she replied.

FUNNY THING, GETTING OLDER

For many years, I thought about what she said and became more and more interested about the lives of the people and the children on both sides of the struggle in the Middle East. I think it was a documentary about the walls the Israelis were building on the West Bank and around Gaza that first gave me the idea for a story I might write. After a while, it became a story I needed to write, had to write.

I come from a generation that witnessed in the 1960s the construction of another wall, a wall that divided the world and brought us to the brink of destruction, as this one still might.

Difficult to imagine, but the Cold War once seemed just as intractable as the conflict in the Middle East does now. Then one day in Berlin, quite suddenly, it seemed at the time, people simply decided enough was enough and tore the wall down. Surely the same thing will happen one day in Israel and Palestine. So, in that hope, I wrote my story of the children living either side of the wall, their lives already scarred by tragedy. I called it *The Kites Are Flying*.

Told in part by Max, a journalist visiting the Palestinian side of the wall for the first time, it is the story of Said, a young shepherd boy who has not spoken a word since he witnessed the death of his brother, killed by an Israeli soldier while out flying his kites. Said becomes obsessed with the making of kites and when the wind is right, sends them off over the wall to an Israeli girl in a wheelchair – injured when her family car was blown up by Palestinians and her mother killed. Each of Said's kites has a message of peace written on it.

At the end of the story, Max is about to leave Said for the last time. Said is sitting on the hillside making his next kite, with his sheep all around him. This is what happens:

I was just about organised and ready to film him again when Said sprang to his feet. The sheep were bounding away from him, scattering over the hillside. Then I saw the kites. The sky above the Israeli settlement was full of them, dozens of them, all colours and shapes, a kaleidoscope of kites. Like butterflies they danced and whirled around each other as they rose into the air. I could hear shrieks of joy, all coming from the other side of the wall. I saw the crowd of children gathered there, every one of them flying a kite. Then, one after the other, the kites were released and left to the wind, and on the wind they flew out over the wall towards us. From behind us now, from Said's village, the people came running out as the kites began to land in amongst us, and amongst the terrified sheep too. Uncle Yassa picked up one of them. 'You see what they wrote? Shalom,' he said. "They wrote, Shalom. Can you believe that?'

All around me, Said's family and many of the other villagers, mothers and fathers, grandmothers and grandfathers, began to clap, hesitantly at first. But I noticed then that it was only the children who were whooping and whistling and laughing. The hillside rang with their jubilation, with their exultation. It seemed to me like a glorious symphony of hope.[3]

Sentimental clap-trap, I hear you thinking. Maybe, or rather a hope that a new generation will one day rise above the prejudice and suspicion, hurt and hatred – as has happened in Europe, in South Africa, in Ireland and in Egypt. Each a process of reconciliation that's still ongoing, of course. It is the children of today, yesterday and tomorrow who will do this also in Israel and Palestine, given half a chance.

During the Israeli incursion into Gaza of 2008, according to Amnesty International, 300 Palestinian children were killed. And yes, I know Hamas rockets had been landing in Israel for a very long time and that Israeli children have been dying there too. And I know it is absolutely the right of every nation to defend itself. So most certainly the Israelis have had their reasons. But I'm sure that most of them believe as we all do that a child's life in particular is precious, any child's life. Yet Palestinian children died. Collateral damage, some might call it.

And then, sometime after I wrote my book, I was asked by Save the Children to become an ambassador for them, to go to the Middle East, to see the work they are doing in Israel and Gaza, and to find out whether there is in reality any cause for hope. I went there in 2010. I wanted to hear the children's stories on both sides of the wall, to tell my own stories, to make kites and maybe even fly them if we could.

First, I spent two days in Israel. I visited Neve Shalom/Whakat As-Salam, a co-operative village school, bilingual, bi-national, the first such school in the country. Here, Arab and Jewish children play together and learn together. I wanted to know what they thought, how they felt about one another. We made kites and we flew them, and on the kites they had written – without any prompting from me – their own messages of peace.

Next to Tel Aviv, to a meeting organised by Windows for Peace, a forum where Israeli and Palestinian teenagers can come together to try to reach some understanding of the point of view of the other side, however difficult that may be. There was obvious resentment and hurt, but no anger, no bitterness. The very fact that these young people were there together, and talking, seemed to me to be hopeful. I learnt from them that both communities felt hemmed in, caged in – the Israelis by the states that surround them and threaten their very existence, and the Palestinians by the walls the Israelis have built and the takeover of their land, the building of settlements. With the best will in the world, I could see it would be a long time before Israeli and Palestinian kids would be flying kites over these walls. It would take time, they said. Maybe their grandchildren would see peace. 'No,' said one of them, 'I think it'll be my grandchildren's grandchildren before they'll fly the kites. But there will be peace one day.'

Then came my two days in Gaza. Just getting in was a nightmare. Gaza itself is a narrow strip of land, only eight kilometres wide in places and barely forty kilometres in length. Until you see the place for yourself, you can't imagine it. The land and its people are under siege, imprisoned, with the wall on three sides and blockaded by warships out at sea. Even if you're with Save the Children, I discovered, you might not get in. To my dismay, my companion, Kate Redman, was turned back by Israeli border guards. No reason was given. The Gaza crossing seemed designed to isolate and maybe even to humiliate. There were rigorous questions about my

SET OUR CHILDREN FREE

intentions in Gaza, my bags were rummaged through and then, at last, I was allowed through into a 100-metre-long steel tunnel – it was like a set from *Doctor Who*. I was alone, except for the surveillance cameras watching me. Then I was out into a walkway, about two kilometres long, completely caged in, with a kind of no-man's-land, a blasted wilderness of rubble and ruin stretching out as far as the eye could see, on either side of me. Halfway down, I heard the sound of a shot being fired – it sounded to a country boy like me as if someone was shooting rabbits.

All around, young Palestinian boys were racing around on their donkeys and carts whooping and shrieking. I had no idea what they were doing at the time. I was in another world. I didn't know who was doing the shooting.

In this other world, I went the next day to visit a hospital for malnourished babies and then on to a project for blind children. I thought these children had something in common with those at Yarl's Wood. They were walled in, imprisoned.

A robin redbreast in a cage
Puts all Heaven in a rage.

I went to talk to children in a school in Gaza City, to make kites again, to fly them, but sadly not over any wall. I discovered no one is allowed within 300 metres of the wall that surrounds Gaza. But we made kites all the same. Some of them wrote on their kites 'Rights and Peace'. Hamas, who controls what can and cannot happen in Gaza, would not allow boys and girls to fly their kites together on the beach, I was told. So we went to a park, the only green space I saw in Gaza City; 'Le Jardin de Paris' it was called.

Here I flew kites with the children. There was more laughter than wind, but that was fine. A day or so later, on my way out of Gaza, I found myself waiting at the Palestinian Authority barrier. The reason we had to wait was that the border had been closed. Only an hour ago, two boys had been shot close to the wall.

All around me, I saw those youngsters again, hundreds of them, out with their donkeys and carts collecting rubble and gravel to be recycled for building blocks in Gaza City – no new building materials are allowed in. Earlier that morning, before I got there it seemed, some of the scavengers had ventured too close to the wall and had been fired at and wounded. I waited in the heat for long hours, watching the kids at work, coming and going with their donkeys and carts. They didn't seem worried, so I wasn't worried. I just wanted to get out of this place.

It was then I heard shots, then screaming, saw the kids running to help their wounded friends. Now I really was outside the comfort zone of fiction. A doctor from Médecins Sans Frontières waiting there with me told me that the shots were probably not fired by marksmen from the watchtowers on the wall, but that these scavengers were sometimes targeted, remotely, electronically, from Tel Aviv, which was miles away – 'Spot and Strike', they call it. Like a video game – a virtual shooting. I don't know if these claims are true but I do know the shots were real. There was blood, the boy's trousers were soaked in it. The bullets were real. I saw him close to, saw his agony as the cart rushed by me.

Many like him, the doctor said, ended up maimed for life. Here was a child, imprisoned and under siege, being deliberately targeted, his right to survival, the most basic of all children's rights, being utterly ignored.

When I think about it, it isn't just the shock and horror of that one terrible moment that I remember. What will live with me as well are the voices of the children I met, the stories they told me: the blind boy who said his greatest wish was to worship at the mosque in Jerusalem, and a girl in the same group who told me that it wasn't the Israeli children that she hated, but the soldiers. She wanted to be friends with Israeli children. Her greatest wish? 'Freedom,' she said, 'and peace.'

FUNNY THING, GETTING OLDER

So, when on my return I was asked to give this lecture, I knew immediately that I would take this opportunity to speak out about the rights of all children everywhere. I'm sure some people will accuse me of taking sides in this conflict but let me make it quite clear that I am simply on the side of the children, all of them, from whichever country – for children in any conflict are always the innocent victims. It is not children who make wars.

It's all too easy for each of us to feel helpless when we witness such appalling treatment, such flagrant abuse of children's rights. But if ever we think that one voice can't make a difference, then remember, that if it hadn't been for the campaign against Yarl's Wood – single voices added together – children would still be imprisoned there.

Those people helped to set those children free.

We have to set our children free, all of them, wherever they are – free to enjoy their childhood, to live in peace and security, free from poverty, disease and ignorance.

This last brings me to education, by no means the least of the rights of the child. For me, it is one of the most fundamental. In this respect, we should ask the question: are we doing the best for children in our schools here at home? The answer is, I'm afraid, that we are not, that far too many of our children are failing, which means we are failing our

SET OUR CHILDREN FREE

children. And we are responsible for that, not just government and teachers, who are blamed constantly, but all of us.

Time for another story – I'll tell you why afterwards. It's one that I heard in Russia in 2003. There was an extraordinary happening to which I was invited, a gathering of 400 librarians from all over Russia. On my first evening in Moscow, I found myself in the Kremlin, a glittering palace of gold and white, buzzing with people talking about books. It was a great, celebratory evening, the kind of glitz that you would never find at a conference for librarians in England – more's the pity. (Think of that in a month when we're told hundreds of libraries across Britain might have to close.) In fact, it was a celebration of librarians – the unsung heroes of the book world – of the importance of the work they do in bringing books to children and children to books. So this was dear to my heart.

Instead of a cabaret, there was a prize giving. And right at the end of a rather long evening, the last prize winner was announced. As he stood up, a rather diminutive man in an ill-fitting suit, 400 librarians rose to their feet and began huzzah-ing like Russian troops at Borodino. I turned to my minder and asked her what was so special about him. Ah, she said, he is a hero. One day, his library caught fire. With no thought for his own safety, he rushed into the building and began to carry out armfuls of books. Inspired by his courage and determination, the townspeople followed suit, so that before the building burned to the ground, they had saved about three quarters of the books in the library – thousands of them.

'And the story doesn't end there,' she said. 'He told the townspeople to take the books home and look after them, as many as they could, and then when the library was rebuilt, as he was sure it would be, then they could bring them all back. And that is exactly what happened.' So, with tears in my eyes, I huzzah-ed along with the rest of them.

And I was thinking, it is people like this Russian school librarian who make a real difference to children's lives – a different kind of hero, unfamous, unglamorous. His love of books and his ability to inspire reminded me of the people who had made a difference to my life. My mother reading to me the stories and poems she loved: Kipling, de la Mare, Masefield, Edward Lear; my choir master at school, Edred Wright, whose enthusiasm gave me a lifelong love of music. We can each of us remember the individuals who made the difference in our own young lives. Yet, something is wrong here and it is this: so often, the importance of these individuals in children's lives is not reflected by their importance in our society.

SET OUR CHILDREN FREE

I'm not thinking here simply of the financial rewards, although that is part of the problem. Whether we are talking about people who work in children's theatre, children's television and radio programmes, children's films or children's books, it is the same. You are at the bottom of the pile. It's just for children. And within these worlds, the younger the children concerned, it seems, the less status there is for those involved.

The teaching profession itself is the most obvious example of this. We all know how important those early years are, in or out of school. Yet, those teaching our infants and primary school children are the worst paid in the profession and held in least esteem. So what inevitably happens, of course, is that so many of the most talented young graduates are not just diverted away from teaching altogether because of its lack of status or lack of financial incentive – but in particular from teaching our youngest children, in the very schools where they are needed most, where they can do most good. A pound spent in the early years can save ten pounds later.

But the truth is that because of the nature of our political system, with its short-term, target-driven mindset, we change what happens in education only superficially, usually so that it can be measured within the lifetime of a government. We endlessly jiggle the system and call it reform. I think we have to go back to the child, back to basics – and I do not mean the three Rs, though they are important of course – I mean something very different.

At the heart of every child, new born, is a unique genius and personality. What we should be doing is to allow the spark of that genius to catch fire, burn brightly and shine. What we seem to be doing with so many of our children is to corral them, to construct a world where success and failure are all that count. Fear of failure is what does the most damage.

Back to stories again, to Dickens and Mr Gradgrind in *Hard Times*, whose notion of education was to ram facts into children's heads. We may not beat children any more, and that is progress of course, but sometimes I'm not sure how far we've moved on since Gradgrind or since I was at school myself in the 1950s. We still have classes that are twice the size they should be, far too big for teachers to form those relationships with children that are so important, particularly with those children who are already disengaged and alienated. And we still have a society where, although some schools are wonderfully successful, others remain mired in poverty and failure, a situation which continues to wreck the lives of so many of our children and exacerbate divisions in our national life. It is those schools and those children we are not reaching and whose rights we are denying.

Take New Zealand, a country that's not at all keen on school league tables but somehow managed to rank fourth in the world in the OECD education ratings in 2010. Here, a child begins school on his or her fifth birthday. They do not arrive in bunches of 30 at the beginning of the school year, but as individuals, so that teachers have a chance to get to know each child properly, to build a relationship. I'd prefer it if they went to school a couple of years later as they do in Finland, which, incidentally ranks second in world tables. There they consider that the first seven years of a child's life are best spent at home. I think they find that a child then goes more willingly to school, more prepared, confident and less frightened, perhaps. And before you ask, the UK came twentieth in the same OECD world table.

We must remember that we are preparing children not simply for employment (though that is important) and for the contribution they can make to the common good (which is also important), but for the difficult decisions they will have to make in their personal lives, in those moments when they have to take responsibility for themselves and others, when they decide whether or not to have sex with someone new, to be tempted into drugs, bully a school mate on the internet, carry a knife or throw a brick through a window. In those critical moments, their decisions, the choices they take, rely so much on the relationships they made when they are young – with their parents and their teachers – and on their self-worth and self-confidence. There is no league table for relationships.

Let me tell you another story, this time set in France. I think it's worth telling because it is about the making of friendships, the building of relationships.

We were invited, Clare and I, to Apt, in the Luberon region of France – it's a hard life! – to help with a school project. This is what they were doing: they had in their college a group of disenchanted and hostile teenagers and were trying to find ways of engaging them, of making them feel involved and needed. They had formed an alliance with a local old people's home. Every one of these teenagers had 'adopted' one of the old people, and they would all go up and see them two or three times a week, and simply talk, or walk, just be with them.

Alongside this, the children were encouraged to read stories about relationships between old people and young people, and that's where I came in. I'd written several books where this kind of relationship was central to the plot and many had been translated into French. '*Cher* Monsieur

SET OUR CHILDREN FREE

Morpurgo, come and read to the children,' they wrote to me, 'and talk to them, and hear what they have to say, and listen to what they write.' So we went.

It wasn't easy. Their body language was aggressive but at least they seemed to be listening – perhaps because of our funny accents. They did not talk easily about their relationships with their newly adopted old folk, or about anything else much. But what worked wonderfully well was that young and old were encouraged to meet on their own, away from school. The young people had been allowed to go off piste and had been shown they were trusted.

On the last evening I was there, these previously diffident youngsters read out the poems and stories they'd written about their new friends. The event was held bizarrely in a wine merchant's warehouse. There was a large audience of family and friends there to hear them, amazement writ large on every face. You could have heard a pin drop. The teenagers meant every word they'd written. The friends they'd made up at the old people's home mattered to them. They cared.

My time with those children and teachers in Apt reminded me again that the most important thing in a child's life is the quality of the relationships they make, whether at home or at school, with parents, grandparents, teachers, librarians, whoever. So let's not distract ourselves endlessly with what we call our schools – academies, charter schools, free schools, comprehensives. Forget league tables and targets, and let's break free of the shackles of a narrow curriculum; it's time to focus on the commitment and talent of the people who touch our children's lives.

We have wonderful, motivated, knowledgeable teachers out there – I've met hundreds of them. I've also met many who are not so wonderful, and sometimes that's because they don't have the confidence to be wonderful. They need self-worth too. They need training well, that's for sure. But most of all, they need to have a love of their subject, so that they mean it when they teach it. That's what the children will pick up on.

I have been to many schools up and down the country, and have found children there who love reading. Why? Because they have teachers who have a passion for reading themselves and want to pass it on.

But we can't leave it all to the teachers. If we are to do our best for our children we have to get involved, and the teachers have to allow us to get involved. Let's have more writers, poets and storytellers in schools, along with artists, musicians, dancers, scientists and wizards of technology, sportsmen and women – it is these people, along with the teachers, who will make the difference and change lives. So let's find the funds to do it, even if we are in the grip of austerity. Let's have more trips to theatres and concert halls and museums. Let's get children out into the open air, tramping the hills, sailing the lakes, whatever. All of this should be an integral part of their education, a right, not an extra. It will pay dividends in the end.

And why not, for instance, give over a part of every school day – the last half hour perhaps, when everyone is tired out anyway – simply as a time for reading stories, no questions asked afterwards, no comprehension tests. Call it 'Dreamtime'. Call it what you will. And let's get thousands more grandparents and parents in to listen to children reading, and to tell their stories too. What we absolutely do not need is to be closing down our libraries, cutting back youth services and provision for children with special educational needs. Can we not see the collateral damage that will do to young lives? Let's give them the time and the freedom to dream, to learn – yes, and to fly their kites. Our children are our seedcorn. They have only one chance to grow and they need all the help they can get. We have to be there to give them that help.

One last story. An example of how one individual can enrich our children's lives. There are hundreds of thousands of such people up out there, unnoticed for the most part, doing their best for our children. This last story is sung in praise of all of them, and of one in particular.

I live down a deep lane in Devon near a project whose work is close to my heart. For children, our charity Farms for City Children is an experience, like a great book, a great play, a great symphony, that opens their eyes to new possibilities and fresh hope. It also gives them a sense of belonging and responsibility. Here's what one of our neighbours, the poet Sean Rafferty, wrote. He used to see the children out at work on the farm every day.

> *Now more than ever it matters that children from the inner-cities can experience life in the country. This is a generation that will hear repeatedly of ecological disaster; will be told that the earth itself is threatened. For some of them the earth will not be a globe in the classroom or a map on the wall but a Devon farm where they scuffled beech leaves along the drive and broke the ice on the puddles in the lane. When they are told of polluted rivers it will be one river, which has had its share of pollution, where they first saw a trout jumping and a wading heron, and plastic bags caught in the branches to mark the level of the last great flood. Last spring, two children went*

down to the river at dusk to watch for badgers. They did see a badger and they also saw two young otters at play, something many people born and bred in the country have never seen. It was as though Nature herself were choosing her champions.[4]

Only poets can write like that – even if it was prose. In my next life, I think I'm going to be a poet, if I can't be an albatross or an elephant, that is. But in this life, at least, I shall continue to tell the story, sing the anthem, and speak up for the needs and rights of children as best I can.

PEACE AND WAR

LUCY LOST

2014

I wrote a book called Listen to the Moon *in 2014. My working title was 'Lucy Lost'. The* Lusitania *was always known as 'Lucy'.*

Over the next four years of the centenary of the First World War, there will be one or two well-known dates, a few anniversaries of iconic battles, thoughts of some names and places – Ypres, Arras, Loos, maybe – or a familiar object will surface in the house, a medal perhaps, with a story to go with it. And all of these will be markers for us, pointers, reminders, a hundred years later, of lives lived then, of deeds done, of deaths died. Some will be personal: the date of a great-grandfather's death, a faded photo of his name in Portland stone at the Bedford House Cemetery near Ypres, a stained letter scribbled in pencil or one of those brass Christmas boxes, full of chocolate or cigarettes, presented by Princess Mary to the troops at the front at Christmas 1914 and passed down through the family from some distant but now long-forgotten relative. The poems of Owen,

Sassoon, Blunden and Thomas will be read rather more, might mean rather more.

One date, as we all know, has come and gone already: 4 August 2014, the centenary of the declaration of war at 11 o'clock at night. For some, the next significant date may well be 1 July 2016, one hundred years since the first day of the Battle of the Somme. Some 20,000 British men died that day. And many of us will know when the guns at last fell silent, at 11 o'clock on the morning of 11 November 1918. It was the day peace began. Or was it just half-time?

A date less familiar to many will come next year, on 7 May 2015, one hundred years after the sinking of the RMS *Lusitania* by a German U-boat. It happened 12 miles south of the Old Head of Kinsale, off the coast of Ireland, in bright sunshine and calm seas.

I know about this only because I have just written a story about it, a novel I should never have thought of writing in the first place had I not, years ago, come across a medal handed down through the family. It is not a medal for bravery but rather a badge of shame, a medal designed and made by the German side to celebrate and proclaim a great and destructive naval triumph. It was then reproduced in vast numbers by our side, as evidence of German brutality, in a war that was full of propaganda and counter propaganda – as wars of course have always been. The difficulty, then as now, is in discovering the truth behind the propaganda. Nearly a hundred years later, the truth still lies deep in murky waters off the Old Head of Kinsale.

None of this was of any interest whatsoever to a small child of six years old, who, in the summer of 1948, had caught chickenpox. Finding herself isolated in the guest room far from the rest of the household and already feeling better, she was becoming increasingly bored. She climbed naughtily out of her sickbed and, for no good reason, began to rummage around in the back of the chest of drawers. She was the one who discovered the medal, hidden away under some of her father's old socks.

This little girl was Clare, now my wife of 60 years! The guest room and the chickenpox she remembers only vaguely. But the shock of her discovery at the back of the chest of drawers is vivid still. It was, she says, a large, dark-looking medal, a thing of gloomy shadows, heavy to hold in a small hand and rather rusty. Then she saw what the shadows were. On one side of the medal, depicted in relief, was a great ship going down under the waves, a scene of dreadful devastation to her. The ship appeared to be carrying guns and shells, even a warplane. But on the reverse side was an image even more horrifying to the little girl. Passengers were queueing up to

FUNNY THING, GETTING OLDER

buy their tickets for the ship from the skeletal figure of Death, a skull for a head. The words above this hideous image, *Geschäft über alles* ('business above everything'), would of course have meant nothing to her at the time. She was as fascinated as she was horrified, and replaced this grim discovery back under her father's socks, taking it out to look at again only when she could summon up the courage to do so.

I know all this because some years later, when she and I had met and married, her father gave us that chest of drawers to help us set up home. We found the medal still there, hidden away, the skull still grinning. It turned up from time to time after that, an uncomfortable and disturbing presence, but one that would not be ignored. I needed to find out more about it.

It was, I discovered, one of 300,000 such medals produced by Selfridges of London to be sold widely for charity, deliberately to counter the German claim that the *Lusitania* had been carrying armaments as well as passengers as she crossed the Atlantic, and that, as a ship of war, they had every right to sink her.

But these medals were copies of a German original. The German sculptor, Karl Goetz, enraged that a passenger ship should have been used by the British in this underhand way, and that Germany should find herself condemned by the whole world for the terrible loss of life, had produced 500 medals to celebrate the sinking of the great liner, making it quite explicit in the design that she was carrying weapons of war, that Cunard, the ship's owners, knew this, and that in selling tickets for the crossing, they were putting business before the lives of their passengers. *Geschäft über alles.*

The British cleverly turned this triumphalist sentiment on its head, citing it as evidence yet again of German callousness and barbarism. As it turned out, this war of the medals was a propaganda war that the British won. In the end this was to prove vital to the Allied cause and make a significant contribution to final victory.

I wanted answers to questions, to sort out the facts of a history so corrupted by propaganda. To do this, I needed to know all I could of the German U-boat campaign in the Atlantic in the early years of the First World War, and to find out as much as possible about the sinking of the *Lusitania*. It was not easy. Archive material of the time – newspapers, even film – helped hugely, but was often tainted with the prejudices of the time, on both sides. But the more I read and researched, the more the fog of war lifted.

The dominance of the seas by the surface ships of the Royal Navy in 1914 was such that the blockade of German ports was almost total, depriving Germany of much of the food and materials she needed to keep her people fed and to fight the war effectively. The port of Ostend was her only access to the Channel, the North Sea and the Atlantic, and it was largely from here that the Imperial German Navy sent out her U-boats. Her aim was to do to Britain what Britain was doing to Germany: starve the country of the supplies she needed to sustain her people and to conduct the war effort. Much of these supplies came from America. The early U-boats were few in number and slow, blind under the surface, but they were undetectable. They very soon began to wreak havoc amongst naval and merchant shipping, causing appalling losses in men and ships. (In total, German U-boats sunk almost 5,000 ships, in all 13 million in tonnage. The price they paid was terrible. They lost 178 boats and 5,000 crew.)

As the struggle intensified at sea, the Germans declared a 'war zone' around the coast of Britain and Ireland. Any ships sailing in these waters, neutral or not, were now liable to attack. It was unrestricted submarine warfare. By 1915, the U-boats were threatening to cut Britain off from her supply line and bring her to her knees. At one point, ships were being sunk at the rate of two a day.

One of the ships was auxiliary cruiser HMS *Bayano*, which was torpedoed on 11 March 1915 and sank within three minutes. There was great loss of life. The wireless operator, Walter Lloyd, stayed at his post and sent off an SOS message. He died doing his duty.

At the beginning of May, the Middlesbrough steamer *Edale* was torpedoed off the Isles of Scilly but in this instance, the U-boat captain gave warning so that the crew could get off before she was attacked. No lives were lost.

There were casualties though when the American oil tanker SS *Gulflight* was torpedoed off the Bishop Rock Lighthouse. The captain and two sailors died. They were Americans, neutrals. America was outraged. There was greater outrage to follow, from both sides of the Atlantic.

On 23 April 1915, the German embassy put a notice in several newspapers in New York, which were often placed alongside advertisements for the *Lusitania*'s next Atlantic crossing. Despite these warnings, RMS *Lusitania*, commanded by Captain William Turner, sailed from New York at noon on 1 May with 1,959 passengers and crew on board. She was a grand ship and had once held the Blue Riband for the fastest crossing of the Atlantic.

The voyage across the Atlantic was uneventful. Precautions were taken as they entered the war zone: watertight doors were closed, lookouts posted and a blackout was imposed on the night of 6 May. The lifeboats were swung out on their davits and made ready, in case. On the morning of 7 May, there was heavy fog and more lookouts were posted. The speed, already reduced for reasons of economy, was reduced even further, to 15 knots. Close now to the Irish coast, the ship's foghorn was sounded, which alarmed some of the passengers – many were well aware that there was a danger of attack by submarines and this might reveal to an enemy where the ship was. At 10 a.m., the fog lifted and by noon it was clear. They were now in bright sunshine and passing through calm seas.

U20, captained by Walther Schwieger, spotted the funnels of the *Lusitania* at 1.20 p.m. Schwieger set a course to intercept. At 2.10 p.m., he fired one torpedo at a range of 700 metres. The torpedo hit the starboard side behind the bridge.

In Schwieger's words, recorded in his log: 'The explosion of the torpedo must have been followed by a second one (boiler or coal or powder?) . . . The ship stops immediately and heels over to starboard very quickly . . . The name *Lusitania* becomes visible in golden letters.'

One passenger later reported that when the torpedo hit, 'it sounded like a million-ton hammer hitting a steam boiler a hundred feet high'.

The second, more powerful explosion sent a geyser of water, coal, dust and debris into the sky.

LUCY LOST

An SOS was immediately sent out and received 12 miles away on the Irish coast. Electrical power failed, plunging the interior of the great ship into darkness. It was listing already 15 degrees to starboard. The order to abandon ship was given. There were 48 lifeboats on board, enough for everyone, but there was not time to fill them and get everyone safely into the water. The ship sank in 18 minutes. It took some hours for help to arrive. Many had already drowned in the cold water, but 764 passengers and crew were rescued and landed at Queenstown, now Cobh, near the city of Cork.

In all, 1,195 had been lost and of these only 289 bodies were recovered. They were buried in Kinsale and Queenstown. Amongst them were more than 120 American citizens, including the writer Justus Forman, millionaire Alfred Vanderbilt and philosopher Elbert Hubbard.

That Walther Schwieger knew what he was doing when he fired that torpedo there can be little doubt. The ship was instantly recognisable. He believed she was a legitimate target, a passenger ship being used surreptitiously as a ship of war. And the Germans had made it plain that they had every intention of sinking her. But he must have known there were nearly 2,000 people on board – women, children, families, British and American. He also knew she was unarmed and posed no threat to his ship. The convention – not always adhered to – was that unarmed ships should be warned before they were sunk, so that passengers and a crew had a chance to get away in lifeboats. It was a common enough practice carried out by many U-boat commanders. He chose to give no such warning.

The printed warning that had appeared in American papers before the sailing, however, acquired an ominous tone in retrospect.

There followed claims and counter claims, the Germans insisting the *Lusitania* was 'carrying large quantities of war material in her cargo' and that she was classed officially as 'an auxiliary cruiser'.

The truth? Difficult. It is certainly true that RMS *Lusitania* had once been classified as an auxiliary cruiser at the beginning of the war, but she had been declassified and the Germans knew it. It is true also that the *Lusitania* was carrying small arms cartridges in large numbers. These munitions were on the manifest, but this was not made known at the time to the public in Britain. These cartridges were not for shooting grouse, I suspect.

We can think what we like. There was hypocrisy and skulduggery on both sides. But it was Schwieger who sent that torpedo away. The fact is that two years after this tragedy, the United States joined the war on the Allied side. Had they not done so, it is likely that the outcome of the First World War would have been very different.

Our own *Lusitania* medal tells a terrible tale. A hundred years on, there are still unanswered questions, that's for sure. I myself have often asked a different kind of question: why was that medal hidden away in a sock drawer in my wife's family home? I think I may know the answer. But it is only supposition. Lt Commander John Lane, beloved brother of Clare's father Allen Lane, was killed six months after Clare was born in 1942. His ship, HMS *Avenger*, was torpedoed in the Mediterranean by a German U-boat. There were Swordfish aircraft on deck. He died with 516 others. Only 12 were saved. Allen Lane was devastated by the loss. I think someone in the family never wanted him to have to look at that medal again and hid it away.

My novel, *Listen to the Moon*, is supposition. All novels are. It is the story of one survivor from the sinking of the *Lusitania*, a young girl who manages to swim to the ship's piano and use it as a life raft. But here too there is perhaps an element of truth. Three hours or so after the *Lusitania* went down, the grand piano from that luxurious liner was found floating in the sea – in some reports, with a child still clinging on. There are some things you can't make up.

THE TILTH OF TRUTH

2015

I had not intended to write another book set in the First World War. I had done quite enough of that, I thought, with *War Horse, Private Peaceful, Listen to the Moon, A Medal for Leroy* and *The Best Christmas Present in the World*. I needed to move on, find other times and landscapes to explore. I had lived in the mud and the trenches long enough, witnessed in my mind's eye the suffering of men and horses, the last night of a soldier's life before the firing squad at dawn, the sinking of the *Lusitania*, the life and death of the first Black officer in the British army, the Christmas truce of 1914. Like an old soldier, maybe, I was tired of war, particularly that war.

Then I heard a story which, once told, would not leave me. I had to tell it – it had to be told. I really tried not to write it but it insisted. It is nothing new for me to take historical truth and make my fiction from it. Indeed, I am not sure I have ever written a story that did not have its roots in historical facts, perhaps in my memory or in someone else's. I need to ground my stories in the tilth of truth, to grow them, dream them up

THE TILTH OF TRUTH

that way. But in no story I have written have I needed to stray so little from historical truth as in *An Eagle in the Snow*.

My friend Dominic Crossley-Holland, head of history at the BBC, phoned me and said he had come across a story that he was very excited about. Could he come and talk to me about it with a view to some kind of collaboration? Over a cup of tea a few weeks later, he told me about the story he had discovered. It was the life story, he said, of Henry Tandey VC, the most decorated private of the First World War. My heart sank. Then he began to tell me the story.

Henry Tandey was born in 1891, spent some time in an orphanage, joined the army at the age of 14 and was sent overseas to serve in South Africa. In 1914, at the outbreak of the war, his regiment was ordered to France and Henry Tandey found himself in action for the first time. It soon became clear to all his comrades-in-arms that there was something very special about this young man: he was remarkably brave. Time after time, he rescued people under fire. Time after time, he led attacks on German positions, and time after time, he steadied everyone around him and held ground against repeated enemy attacks. He put himself repeatedly in harm's way and was wounded often, but seemed to lead a charmed life. He was, by all accounts, modest and quiet, unassuming and unwilling to be promoted.

FUNNY THING, GETTING OLDER

He was at one time made a lance corporal but didn't care for it, so demanded to be a private again. He was awarded medal after medal for his courage in the face of enemy fire.

All this would be remarkable enough, but there are many such stories of brave men, of all ranks, on all sides. Though we tend to know more about the lives of those who were the great poets or the great generals. Stories of private soldiers are told usually in citations for medals or on memorial plaques in churches, perhaps. Most are lost in the fog of history. It is likely that Henry Tandey, despite his medals, might have been largely forgotten, but for something that happened at the Battle of Marcoing in September 1918. It was in this battle that Tandey was to win his Victoria Cross, by knocking out German machinegun posts, killing many enemy soldiers and capturing several others, then enabling his comrades to cross a canal by repairing a bridge under fire. It was after the battle was over that a lone German soldier appeared out of the smoke. They were about to shoot him when Tandey stopped them. He simply waved the German away and told him to go home. He spared his life. All this was recorded at the time.

After the war, Tandey went to Buckingham Palace to receive his VC and was famous for a while. He found a job in the Standard Motor Company in Coventry and went back to

THE TILTH OF TRUTH

a normal life. He married but had no children. And that should have been the end of the story. However, in 1934, the chancellor of Germany, Adolf Hitler, began talking about how his life had been spared by a British soldier at the Battle of Marcoing. The soldier concerned, it was claimed, was Private Henry Tandey, recognised from a photograph of him receiving his VC from King George V at Buckingham Palace. Tandey was told about this claim at the time and said he would have shot him if he'd known.

A couple of years later, a request came from the German embassy in London. The Führer would very much like a copy of an oil painting hanging in the officers' mess of the Green Howards depicting Tandey carrying a wounded man into a field dressing station after the Battle of Marcoing. A copy was made. Then, in 1938, Neville Chamberlain famously went off to try to negotiate a peace with Hitler in Munich. He was taken to Berchtesgaden, Hitler's home in the mountains, and was shown this picture of Tandey on the wall. What was said, no one knows. After Chamberlain returned home triumphant, waving his 'peace in our time' piece of paper at the airport, he apparently rang Tandey to tell him. What was said between them, no one knows.

When war was declared, Tandey, now in his forties, tried to join up. We can imagine why. The army wouldn't have him, no matter how many medals he had. He was too old and still suffering from his wounds. So he joined the civil defence and was in Coventry during the terrible bombing of that city in November 1940. He died, still relatively unknown, in 1977 in Coventry.

I realised that some of this story may well not be true, might have been exaggerated and embroidered. However, just a little research told me that most of it did happen. Yes, Hitler was a fantasist. Yes, it is unlikely that Chamberlain called Tandey on the phone; there is no record of it and car workers didn't usually have a phone at home in the 1930s. So yes, there are possible inconsistencies. Yet at its heart it was true. As true as 300 or more British soldiers executed for cowardice or desertion in the First World War, as true as the sinking of the *Lusitania*, as true as the story of the life and death of Walter Tull, the first Black officer in the British army, as true as the Christmas truce of 1914. All of which had been the source material and the inspiration for previous books.

Here in the story of Henry Tandey, I thought, I might explore the nature of courage, why it is that some people will risk all to save the life of another, will fight on against impossible odds. What made Tandey capable of such extraordinary courage? What was motivating him? And here, too, was a man who, for the best of reasons, makes the fine and noble choice to spare the life of an enemy, only to discover later that this was the worst decision he could have made. How must this man have felt, standing in the rubble and ruins of Coventry, knowing that with one bullet he might have saved his city, his country and all of Europe from this tyrant, whose vicious rage and thirst for power were threatening to engulf the world?

It helped in a way that there might be in the story, as I was told it, already a blurring of fact and invention. It helped, too, that so little is known about the character of Tandey, that his life story is sketchy. I felt I could use Henry Tandey's life as an inspiration for my novel, while acknowledging completely how much my story owes to him.

I begin my telling in a train because of a memory my mother had of travelling with my brother Pieter and me in the Second World War. Our train was strafed by a German fighter and the driver raced into a dark tunnel and stopped, and stayed there till it was safe. I recall nothing of course, being too young, but my mother said that in the carriage people told stories to pass the time, to calm the children down. Not a wedding feast as in *The Ancient Mariner*, not on pilgrimage as in *The Canterbury Tales*, but in the pitch black of a railway carriage in the Second World War.

I liked that idea. I could start.

POPPIES

2018

The drums will be beating, the pipes playing 'Flowers of the Forest'. The bugles will sound the 'Last Post' and a silence will fall with the autumn leaves. Two minutes to remember millions. Bugles break the silence. Reveille sends pigeons flying over the roof tops.

Poppies on every coat, Flanders poppies, blood red. Veterans march past the wreaths of poppies at a measured pace under their banners, heads high, medals glittering in the morning sun. And their wounded comrades are there with them. For so many who have been to war there is a life lived with pain, with enduring grief, with memories that haunt. When the bugles die away, they are left with those memories.

This year, it's exactly one hundred years since the guns fell silent, since the First World War at last came to an end. Europe and the world had bled itself to a standstill, millions upon millions dead and wounded on all sides, entire peoples traumatised. The war to end all wars had ended, but even in the peacemaking afterwards, malign seeds were already being sown for the next conflagration 20 years later, the war that killed more millions, my uncle Pieter among them. I think of Uncle Pieter on Remembrance Sunday, as the bugles play. For me, remembrance is personal.

I learnt in my growing days – long before I ever read Wilfred Owen or Edward Thomas, before I read *All Quiet on the Western Front* or saw *Oh! What a Lovely War* – what war did to buildings, to people, to flesh, to friends and families, to society and country; what war had done to nations and peoples all over the globe. Though it took me time to understand there were millions of Uncle Pieters, of grieving families, millions wounded in body and mind suffering still, and not just in our country, but everywhere. That war, even more than the First World War, had been a holocaust of universal suffering the world over.

I am 75 now. With others of my generation, I still have a tenuous thread of memory of growing up in those post-war years, in a country and a family traumatised by war, but free at last of the fear of invasion. Thanks to those millions, I've lived my life, as most of us have in this country, in comparative peace and prosperity and freedom. I know that if they had not held the line in the First and Second World Wars then we should have been overwhelmed; we should have been at the mercy of tyranny. There would have been no peace, no prosperity, no freedom.

FUNNY THING, GETTING OLDER

They went off to fight for many and complex reasons. Because country called, because pals were going, because it was expected of them, because they were told to. But once fighting, they wanted only to get it over, win and come home to live in peace. They fought, suffered and died then for peace, their peace and ours, not for us to make more war, unless there was absolutely no alternative, unless our freedom was again threatened. That was their great hope, to make a lasting peace, that might end all wars.

Now, after more recent conflicts at home and overseas, in which so many died and have suffered since, and are still suffering, we know how difficult it is to keep this precious peace. Our way of remembering them and their forebears in uniform, and the civilian dead too, is and must be personal.

Wearing the red poppy for me is not simply a ritual, not a politically correct nod towards public expectation. It is in honour of them, in respect and in gratitude for all they did for us. But I wear a white poppy alongside my red one because I know they fought and so many died for my peace, our peace. And I wear both side by side because I believe the nature of remembrance is changing, and will change, as the decades pass since those two world wars.

The names on the gravestones, cemeteries and war memorials will still be there, the bugles will call, the pipes play, but we will no longer be able to remember. They'll all be unknown to us, these dearest ones, these dearest sons and daughters, dearest fathers and mothers, mere names, fading faces in photos and flickering black-and-white film.

But there are ways to reach them, to know them again. We can reconstitute the film, bring them new life in colour, as director Peter Jackson has in his film *They Shall Not Grow Old*. We can tell their stories, as I've tried to do in *War Horse*, *Private Peaceful* and *In the Mouth of the Wolf*. In book, play, music, song and film, we can try to keep the memory alive and stay close to them in the only way now left to us, in our imaginings. This way, we can be reminded of the suffering and pain they lived through, of their courage and camaraderie, and reflect again on the freedom and peace they left us, and so be ever more determined to cherish that legacy, to do all we can to keep the peace, and with it our freedom.

IMAGINE

2018

Close your eyes for a moment and imagine that you are a child alone. You have no place you can call home, no community, no family. All you have are memories, but the memories are a torment to you: memories of terrible suffering, of loss and grieving, of fear and terror, of witnessing man's inhumanity to man, of living with death and destruction all around you. You are overcome with sadness and exhaustion, with cold or heat, you are weakened with hunger and illness. You are hiding from danger, fleeing for your life. All you can do is put one foot in front of the other and walk with others towards hope. Somewhere up ahead, you hear, there is safety and shelter, and food and clean water, and warmth and comfort. So you keep walking, find any boat or lorry or train that will get you there. Just keep going, it is your only hope. There will be a home for you somewhere. There has to be. There will be an end to this.

There are fine examples of how our predecessors have shown great kindness towards the suffering of child refugees. And many are doing that right now, in this country and all

IMAGINE

over Europe. Sadly, there is nothing new about this tsunami of suffering that we have been witnessing in recent times. Children flee their homes for many reasons: war and violence, famine, natural disasters. Millions of people all over the world are being driven from their homes, are becoming wandering exiles, often unwanted, often persecuted. Many of them are children alone.

It is not remembered much these days that at the beginning of the First World War, when the German army invaded Belgium, some 250,000 refugees fled their homes and came across the English Channel to the only place of refuge left to them – for many in small boats, this was a perilous journey. Here they were welcomed in, looked after and cared for. The government responded to the crisis, the people responded, my grandparents amongst them. There were children alone, to be taken in, to be fed and clothed and housed. They went to our schools, our churches, our hospitals, became part of us, part of our community. Most left when Belgium was liberated at the end of the war. Some stayed though and became British, as British as I am. Our grandparents and great-grandparents showed us the way.

Then, more recently, just before the beginning of the Second World War, one of the great men of our country, Nicholas Winton – and his remarkable work was not that well known until comparatively recently – took it upon himself to find a way to save all the Jewish children he could from German-occupied Prague. He realised before many did what fate was awaiting them if they stayed at home in Nazi-occupied Europe. He arranged for a train to bring hundreds of child refugees to this country, where they were looked after in homes and families all over the UK. Other trains followed. In the nine months before the outbreak of war in 1939, approximately 10,000 children were brought out in this 'Kindertransport' programme and saved, children who would have otherwise undoubtedly perished, as most of their families did, in Nazi concentration camps. Many of these children, with no families left to return to, stayed here and lived amongst us, became part of who we are in this country. Nicholas Winton showed us the way.

After that war, as after all wars, there were more refugees on the move – this time, more than there had ever been in the history of Europe. There were displaced persons camps set up all over the continent. Conditions were often harsh but there was international recognition that these people, amongst them thousands of child refugees alone in the world, needed homes and countries to go to. Even in the hard times that followed the end of that war, this country lived up to its responsibilities and opened its doors to about

IMAGINE

100,000 refugees, many of them Poles unable or unwilling to return to their own country, now occupied by the Soviets. For them, this island became a haven of freedom and safety. They settled, became part of us. So that generation showed us the way too. They held out a helping hand to families most in need, children most in need, most vulnerable.

I have seen for myself what can so easily happen when we turn our backs on them. When we think of these children as a nuisance, or a threat, or as an unwelcome intrusion into our so comfortable world; when we excuse ourselves by imagining that wars that happen far away have little to do with us, that we have no responsibility for refugee children from Syria or Iraq or Afghanistan.

A camp full of these children grew and grew like a cancer of misery and rejection outside Calais – 'The Jungle' it was called. But it was no jungle. A jungle is a place where plants and creatures belong and coexist. There is harmony in nature even if it might seem cruel. There was no harmony in the refugee camp, only cruelty. These thousands of young people, many of whom had relatives in the UK and a right to come here, were there because they were seeking a home in our country, a place of safety, and they found themselves corralled behind wire, guarded by French police, victims still of hostility, oppression and deprivation, after all they had been through. They were regularly beaten up by French police. I saw one such case with my own eyes. But we in the UK were complicit in that violence. We were the ones shutting them out.

Visiting that camp, writing about it, raging about it is not enough. Making plays and films about their situation is not enough. That might raise awareness, and that is important, vital. But our forebears did something about it. And indeed, many individuals, Lord Alfred Dubs in particular, but many others too, many charities and organisations, including Safe Passage and the Refugee Council, have been and are doing all they can to welcome these child refugees in.

It shames us that until now, this country has managed to bring over, look after and find homes for only 1,700 of these children. Tens of thousands are still scattered in the cities, towns and villages of Europe, trapped in makeshift camps, sleeping rough, vulnerable to exploitation, homeless. And we have the homes. We have the people too who want to help these children to find a safe and legal way to come and live in our country.

There is a wonderfully imaginative initiative about to happen that will enable all of us to reach out to these refugee children. And our own children can be involved in this too, and how good is that? To engage with the wider world at an early age, to learn empathy and understanding, to know you can make a difference – all these should be part and parcel of a child's education in this ever-more complicated world.

This year, 15 November marks the seventieth anniversary of the meeting in 1938 that precipitated the legislation that allowed the Kindertransport to happen. Safe Passage and all the other agencies concerned are organising a series of events up and down the country starting in September. And here's where the children, our children, and their parents and their schools maybe, come in. The children will be acting out escape – over water, over walls, through fences, overcoming all kinds of obstacles in their way. The adults looking on will offer support, maybe even a little help and advice, to encourage the 'refugee children' to keep going, to reach safety. At the end, the organisations will be asking government to commit to a target of welcoming in 10,000 child refugees over the next ten years. This will be an act of communal caring, a recognition of responsibility on behalf of us all. We have been shown the way. Let's do it, for the refugee children, for ourselves as a people.

THE ROAD TO PEACE

2018

I walked once in no-man's-land, in the countryside outside Ypres and stood in lush farmland where cows grazed. There was a blustery wind, blowing the crows about the sky. I could have been walking the land at home in Devon. But this was the very place where, over a hundred years before, the Christmas of 1914, soldiers on both sides decided to clamber out of their trenches and meet in the middle to wish one another Happy Christmas, *Joyeux Nöel, Frohe Weihnachten.* They shook hands, exchanged gifts of hats and badges, swapped schnapps for whisky, and talked of life in the trenches and of home. Wandering freely about in their greatcoats, they showed family photographs, smoked and laughed, played football together, and all too soon said their goodbyes and drifted apart again, making their way back through the barbed wire to their trenches, where they sang carols to one another long into the night across no-man's-land. The next day, they were doing their best to kill one another again. Not a myth. These things happened.

THE ROAD TO PEACE

This Christmas truce, in many places up and down the hundreds of miles of the Western Front, would be the last time in the four long and hideous years of a catastrophic war which cost so many millions of lives that men walked this no-man's-land with peace and reconciliation in their hearts. Twenty years of uneasy peace followed before Europe erupted into the next world war, bringing yet another holocaust of suffering and grieving and destruction down upon the peoples of the entire world. I was born during that war and lived my childhood with the destruction of the Second World War all about me.

We emerge this November from the centenary of the end of the First World War, from four years of collective reflection on the tragic loss of an entire generation that was, as that great song 'The Green Fields of France' goes, 'butchered and damned'. We have been looking back and remembering – or trying to, because remembering a time and a war that none of us can remember is hard. Our link to those times might be through an old photograph in a family album, or in school records, or on gravestones and memorials. But the faces and names are mostly unknown. Unknown soldiers all now. Their stories are told by the great wartime poets and novelists, and we have historians to guide us through. But the writing that brings me closest to their lives and their deaths are the diaries and the letters. In these, we can hear the spoken word written down. There is no artifice. They tell it as they were living it, in the knowledge that this might be their last day on earth, their last hour, even. We have insight into their darkest fears, their dearest wishes, their fervent hopes. We can discover that, even though they realised full well they might not be there to see the end of the war, there was occasionally a remarkable vision of how the world might be and could be and should be after all the suffering was over.

Because I have written extensively about war and its consequences over the years, I have received several hundred letters from readers, of all ages, telling me the stories of grandfathers and grandmothers who lived through those times, enclosing copies of their letters and diaries, often with photographs. They are always touching – searing in their sadness, life-enhancing in their hope.

But recently, a friend of mine, Tom Heap, shared with me some letters from a great uncle of his that might well help us all find a new way of remembering altogether, a way that will enable millions of us to look forward rather than back. Second Lieutenant Alexander Gillespie, like so many of his generation, was a prolific letter writer. He was killed in 1915, aged 26, just three months after his younger brother, Thomas.

THE ROAD TO PEACE

Both died near La Bassée in France, 'in some corner of a foreign field', and neither of their bodies was ever found. An entire book was later published filled with Second Lieutenant Gillespie's letters. I have not read a more poignant and intimate account of life in the trenches – of longing for home, of the pity and futility of it all, of the courage and the fear and the camaraderie. No work of poetry or fiction, drama or film about that war has moved me more.

Alexander Gillespie's inspired idea, that Tom and now many others would like to make a reality, was first contained in a letter he wrote from the Western Front to his old headmaster at Winchester College, Montague Rendall, on 14 June 1915. These are his words:

There are graves scattered up and down, some with crosses and names upon them, some nameless and unmarked – as I think my brother's grave must be, for they have been fighting round the village where he was killed all through these last eight months. That doesn't trouble me much for 'every soil provides a grave'. But still these fields are sacred in a sense, and I wish that when peace comes, our government might combine with the French government to make one long avenue between the lines from the Vosges to the sea, or, if that is too much, at any rate from La Bassée to

FUNNY THING, GETTING OLDER

Ypres . . . I would make a fine broad road in the No Man's Land between the lines, with paths for pilgrims on foot, and plant trees for shade, and fruit trees . . . A sentimental idea perhaps, but we might make the most beautiful road in all the world.[5]

The French and the Belgians have recently been approached and think highly of the idea. All we have to do now is to make a reality of Alexander Gillespie's magnificent dream. How wonderful it will be to walk along a new pilgrims' way, over the Normandy land, over the ground where so many fought and fell. The trenches and the wire and the craters, all gone; the hate and the fear, all gone. Our children and our children's children will be able to walk through grassy meadows, under spreading trees, and remember that there was once a terrible war here, but now there is a blessed peace they can enjoy, and how it must never be taken for granted.

Postscript
The Western Front Way, the Path of Peace, is now open and can be – and is being – walked, from Switzerland to the sea.

THE PHOENIX OF PEACE

2020

I am not impartial about Europe and I will not pretend I am. Like it or not, and I do like it, I am European. I am British too, British and European. Like many millions all over Britain and Europe, the DNA of my family is a most interesting mix. We are English, Belgian, German, French, Dutch, Croatian, Welsh, Scottish and Romanian. I live in a country where our royal family has its origins in literally dozens of European countries. They are as European as any of us, and more so than most of us.

Our language, arguably the jewel of our culture, is a mongrel language, a magnificent blend from all over the British Isles and all over Europe too – from, amongst others: Scandinavia, Italy and Greece, from France and Germany. Our laws and our early religion have their foundations in Rome, our democracy in Athens. Much of our greatest literature has grown out of a European tradition, European history. Shakespeare found much of his inspiration for his plays from European stories, from *Hamlet* to *Romeo and Juliet* to *Julius Caesar*. And many of the folk tales and legends we love and grow up with – Grimm, Hans Christian Andersen, La Fontaine – have their roots in Europe. We do not need a flag or anthem or even a union to be European. We are European. We share her history, her culture, her learning, her glories and her shames.

Over the centuries, we have been allies, then enemies, then allies again, many times over, too many times over, with just about every country in Europe. We have all done war to death. We are arguably the most belligerent and destructive continent on this earth, the cockpit of the world. If we have one fatal flaw, it is that the nation states of Europe all too often resort to squabbling and fighting to solve problems. And Britain has done its share, been very European in this regard. Like all other countries in Europe, we have invaded and been invaded. We have known the exultation of victory and the humiliation of defeat. And we have known loss and suffering.

Here's the problem, a problem uniquely our own. We are an island. For all our lives, many of us have thought of Europe as being 'over there' or 'overseas'. 'Foreigners' live there. Both geographically and psychologically, we are apart. We always have been. The English Channel separates and protects us, has saved us from invasion, though not always. It is our wall against the world, our shelter and our refuge.

THE PHOENIX OF PEACE

Once upon a time, it was our defence against a hostile world. We could hide behind it, make a fortress of it. Naturally a maritime nation, it was often from the English Channel that we set out to explore the wider world, frequently discovering that other European nations were doing much the same thing – trading, occupying, colonising, converting, creating competing empires. Now we could continue our European squabbling and fighting all over the world.

But thankfully, the days of European empires are gone. These days, we like to use the seas around us for travel and tourism and trade, and fishing. We built a tunnel: we joined Europe physically. And we joined Europe politically. We joined for business, for trade deals. Financially ruined after the Second World War, struggling to recover, profiting less and less from empire, we needed the money, needed the employment. Europe was close, an important market.

Like countries everywhere, we know and understand very little of the history of others. We each see the world through our own prism, our own perspective. We either did not realise or we forgot the reason the European Union, the EEC, the European Community, the Common Market, came into existence and who had created it. A phoenix of peace, inspired by great and good people, was rising from the ashes of the ruins of a Europe that had twice embroiled itself in the most terrible wars the world had ever known. We had dragged the rest of the world into these wars, exporting our special European way of sorting out differences, spreading death and destruction to all corners of the globe.

France and Germany, the two great powers on the European continent, had been warring with one another for three centuries and more before the Second World War, with Britain and others joining in on one side or the other, whichever was deemed right or expedient at the time. After the Second World War, both France and Germany were determined that there should never be another war between them. To ensure this, they would create a trade agreement, a partnership so necessary to both countries that it would make war redundant. Cooperation and mutual benefit would make conflict and enmity a thing of the past. Trade without barriers between democratic nations, freedom of speech and movement, human rights, work and prosperity for all – this was how the new peace in Europe was to be forged.

It was a dream, a hope, a determination. Other European countries liked the sound of this – a Europe of prosperity and peace. Soon it was a community of six European nations. And Britain, after a while, feeling rather left out, decided she wanted to join, that it was in our interest. We wanted a bit of

THE PHOENIX OF PEACE

that prosperity too. Though we were tentative and suspicious. We had only recently been rulers of a quarter of the earth, we were used to doing things our way. And this European Community was not our initiative. We were latecomers to the table of this European family.

Then our application to join was turned down, by France, our historical rival and nearest neighbour across *La Manche*. More humiliation. We discovered we were joining a trading club, with club rules made up already by other countries, that we were going to have to agree to. At the second attempt, we were allowed in, the somewhat grudging seventh member. By now, though, peace, the founding motivation behind the creation of this new European Community or Union had all but been forgotten. The talk was all of fishing quotas, sausages and the ever-burgeoning bureaucracy in Brussels. Britain was always the reluctant relative in the family, still looking outside Europe to the United States and the Commonwealth countries for friendship. We stamped our feet and sulked rather a lot. No! No! No!

We had a referendum in Britain a couple of years after we joined to confirm our decision. Sixty per cent of the people of Britain decided to stay. And stay we did. But did we ever fully embrace the spirit? Did we fly the starry blue European flag? Did we play the magnificent anthem, or was it too

FUNNY THING, GETTING OLDER

German for us, this glorious 'Ode to Joy'? Yes, we did play it, but not too often, and not with much pride in belonging. Did we give much credit to the funds that flowed to Britain from Europe, to our farming, to the neediest parts of our country? Did we have much respect for European human rights? Not really.

All the talk was of the rules and regulations imposed upon us from Brussels, of our laws and powers and sovereignty being superseded by Europe, of how much it was costing to be a member. Resentment grew, directed towards what was often perceived as interference from Europe in our lives, in our national affairs, as well as towards the growing numbers of countries in the club and the inexorable push towards an ever-greater union with Europe.

Then there was the economic crash, the recession and austerity. Many thousands of refugees from war, hunger and poverty were arriving at the southern borders of Europe seeking safety and a better life. Some of them were coming our way. And this was when Britain's Conservative government, afeared that it would be overwhelmed at the polls by hard-right UKIP, decided for its own political reasons to hold another referendum over our country's membership of this European community. It expected to win. It did not. The government seemed unaware how alienated and threatened

THE PHOENIX OF PEACE

and resentful so many millions of our citizens were feeling. They were feeling left out in the cold, abandoned, ignored. As indeed they have been for decades. In the referendum, Europe took the whole blame.

Some blame was justified. The divide between those who have and those who have not is shamefully wide in this country and all over Europe. Europe has presided over this, driven as it is by seeking a prosperity that has not been nearly inclusive enough. The rise of populist nationalism common to all European states is no accident, no coincidence. It is rather a consequence of a system that favours those who feather their own nests rather than creating societies where benefits are more equitably shared. The European Union has itself forgotten its roots, the real reason for its existence.

And we in this country forgot our history, our long tradition of providing refuge for those in greatest need. Do we remember how persecuted Huguenots came here from France long ago, how Jewish people came here over the centuries and made their lives here, how many came from the West Indies, India and Pakistan, from all over the Commonwealth and the world, and how many of us have migrant roots? Do we recall how 'they' have become 'we', how important 'they' and 'we' have been to the culture and economy of this country? Whatever happened to that generosity of spirit, that embrace of Europe and our common humanity? Maybe we forgot that we are in large part a country of migrants, migrants from Europe, from all over the world.

It was natural enough for Britain, the least committed of the European countries, to be the first to break away. We may not be the last if there is not a new renaissance in Europe. Go on as we are and things will fall apart; the centre will not hold. Europe – with Britain still a member, which is my fervent hope – has to remember its history, reinvent itself, reform itself, if it is to survive.

The Union is a voluntary gathering of free and democratic nations. If at the heart of Europe, democracy is compromised – which at present it is – then Europe will fail and should fail. If, instead of the founding spirit of cooperation and friendship, there is, or seems to be, a governance that is remote from the people and perceived to be coercive, even authoritarian, then the spirit of the founding fathers and mothers, who knew and lived through the horrors of war, will fade and die. I do not want that to happen.

If Europe dies, then prosperity will die and our blessed peace will die with it. We must not let that happen. I don't want a divorce. I do not want to be estranged from Europe.

THE PHOENIX OF PEACE

It may be a flawed family, but it's my family. All marriages and partnerships have to be worked at. And I want us in Britain to stay and help make it work.

Let the phoenix of peace rise again and shine. Let her shake the ashes off her wings and fly.

ALL THE WORLD'S A STAGE

2021

Written in lockdown.

I am one of the lucky ones. I'm in work and not entirely isolated. I have the company of Clare, my soulmate, family on Zoom, and we have our blackbird in the garden, with whom we often exchange songs. And we have, unlike many our age, survived. So far. Lucky also, because during these long months of the pandemic, we have spent most of our days doing what we would normally do. Mornings, I'm sitting on my bed writing and Clare's been busy sorting 50 years of life's debris in the attic. We go for a walk in the afternoons and then in the evenings, Clare will maybe read through what I've written. A meal or two in between. The next day much the same. That's been the pattern of our existence. I have, we have, remained just about contented, mostly.

But there is an emptiness inside us – inside many of us, I suspect. I look about me often and think: 'Where are all the people?' Like many writers, I have a double life. Yes, I am usually at home writing. But I'm also out meeting people, going to festivals, bookshops and book launches, listening to other writers and illustrators and storytellers. The one side of my life feeds the other. And because my stories are often read by children, I've been going into hundreds of schools over the years to meet the children, here and all over the world. My last school visit was to my old primary school in London, St Cuthbert with St Matthias, where we had to stay outside because of Covid precautions, so they sat distanced out in the playground whilst I read one of my short stories to them, rather fast so they didn't get too cold.

I love telling my tales, person to person, talking about how they come to be written, encouraging children to a love of reading, to finding their voice as writers. I have such precious memories of these visits. I have been to Jura on the west coast of Scotland, sat in the smallest school I've ever been into, with maybe the best view from a classroom window in the world. I gave my talk, listened to their questions. One question was not a question. I've never forgotten it.

'You're not the first writer to come here, you know,' I was told by one of the children.

'Oh,' I replied, trying not to look or sound too miffed. 'Who else has been before me?'

'George Orwell,' she said. 'And he's quite famous.'

FUNNY THING, GETTING OLDER

I remember too The Mainstreet Trading Company bookshop in St Boswells in the Scottish Borders where I've often been, where we all crowd together, cheek by jowl, in an upper room of a converted barn. I met a lady who was sitting downstairs in the bookshop, who told me how much she had enjoyed the books over the years, but that she was too tired to come up to the event because she was terminally ill. She said she wanted to send me something. A Peace Rose arrived shortly after at my home in Devon, the news of her passing a few weeks later.

You don't forget such things, such people. Books are personal, as are all the arts. Deeply personal. But of course, since the onset of this pandemic, writers can no longer meet their readers. All that has ended, for the moment. I may be able to go on writing but I may not meet readers. I may not tell my tales face to face, hear the laughter, see the tears, experience that wondrous silence when we are all lost in the same story, living it together. That vital and personal connection between us has been ruptured. Until now, when we are denied it, I don't think I truly realised how important this live relationship is for me, and for an audience too. I think I rather took it for granted, worried sometimes that festivals, readings and the like could be all too much about signing and marketing.

ALL THE WORLD'S A STAGE

When the pandemic struck, virtually all public arts events closed down. *War Horse,* the great National Theatre play, had to close in Australia on its world tour. The work stopped, dead. So many theatre friends, music friends, film friends were left high and dry, most unemployed and many in despair. With the first shock of it, their lives – professional, financial and personal – had been instantly torn apart. The lockdown was a tsunami for them, the implications of the destruction caused becoming more and more evident as time passed.

We had a breather then and theatres were planning to open again. Then came another lockdown. Hope was dashed. No theatres, no concert halls, no cinemas, no audience. They, and we, continued to be brutally severed from so much we love and rely on for our intellectual and emotional wellbeing. But the resilience and inventiveness of people in the arts did not die. It didn't and it hasn't. There was much-needed government support to help the arts – not enough, but it keeps some heads, not all, above water. That was and is so important.

But just as vital are the green shoots of revival that have been growing everywhere. There was amongst everyone I know in that world a great desire and a powerful need to get up and get going, to reach audiences somehow. The need

FUNNY THING, GETTING OLDER

was, is, mutual – the deeply human need simply to communicate. We might not be able to do it personally, face to face, but there were other ways. And the way was technology.

A year or so ago, I was invited to go to Newcastle, to Seven Stories, a unique and remarkable hub for children's literature. I'd been before. I love going there. Their dedication and enthusiasm is infectious. But it's a long way from Devon, where I live, and it means staying a night. I talk in their upper room usually, which has an audience capacity of 90. Of course, when the time came, in the middle of the pandemic, I could not get up to Newcastle. They would, they said, arrange the event online instead. I was getting more used to this, talking alone in a room to a little black dot on a screen of an iPad. But I found myself ignoring that, and just talking, reading, telling my stories. And there were little appreciative remarks that came up all the time on my screen, which encouraged me to think I was doing all right.

The best news though came afterwards. Apparently, I had been talking not to 90 people, as I had expected, but to 90,000 all around the world, from Newcastle to Nantes, from Russia to Rochester, from Dublin to Denmark, from Melbourne to Mumbai. This new way may not be personal in the sense that we usually understand the word, we may not be linking arms. But we are linking ideas, and sharing our dreams, on a huge and wonderful scale. And isn't this going to be a way forward for us all, a revolutionary way to bring the creative arts to so many more people all over the country, indeed all over the world – to those who, until now, might have been unreachable either through cost or an accident of geography? Must this not be essential to a brighter future for everyone, part of the positive outcome of this pandemic?

For me, this was a revelation. But clearly, many others in the arts were already aware of the phenomenal potential of such technology. Theatres and actors everywhere have been not 'out there' but working from home, performing to stay alive. Take any one of them. The tiny Barn Theatre in Cirencester, which has come together with four other theatres – the Lawrence Batley Theatre in Huddersfield, the Oxford Playhouse, the New Wolsey Theatre in Ipswich and Theatr Clwyd in Mold – to put on their own version of *The Picture of Dorian Gray*, with Stephen Fry and Joanna Lumley. It's just one show of many that are being performed this way. All kinds of theatre and performance and book events are reviving. As a family, we are booked in to go to the wonderful Gifford's Circus in July. The world is opening up, for audiences and artists alike, maybe on Zoom, maybe outside.

But it's a beginning, a new beginning.

THE VIOLIN OF HOPE

2024

Speech for the Anne Frank Foundation.

I am a war baby, born 5 October 1943. Anne Frank probably died on 31 March 1945. We shared this world for only a few months. Whilst she was hiding in an attic in Amsterdam with family and friends from the Nazis, when she and they were finally being betrayed and taken away to Bergen-Belsen concentration camp to be murdered in the Holocaust like millions of others, I was being looked after in my grandparents' comfortable house in Radlett, outside London, with a garden, surrounded by family. Under threat of the war of course, but I knew nothing of that. I knew nothing of the concentration camps either. I did not know about the evil that men do, that sadly does live after them, if we allow it to.

I must have been 11 or 12 when I first knew anything of Anne Frank or the Holocaust. My family knew about it of course but never told me. Like millions of my generation, and the generations to follow, I learnt about it through reading *Anne Frank's Diary*. Her face was on the opening page looking out at me. She wrote directly to me, confiding in me, telling me how it was to be her, how she was enduring her imprisonment in her attic in Amsterdam – the tedium, the frustration, the dread, the anger, the memories, the friends and relations, the hope, the longing to be free again, for liberation to come. It was her living testimony. And it lives on today.

The last page of her diary is the last we hear of her. She is simply not there any more. We knew before we ever read it that she had died, that these were to be her last words. Once read, it is never forgotten.

It was of course not written to be read by others. She did not know that this was to be her testament, the most personal insight into the life of a spirited but ordinary girl whose name and face was one day to be famous all over the world, was to represent for so many all the wickedness and the waste, the horror, the tragedy, shame and pity of the Holocaust.

For ever afterwards, her life and her death has given me, us, some way of beginning to understand the Holocaust. She was the one of the 6 million we all came to know. Her short life and death remind us of man's inhumanity to man, of the depth of cruelty and depravity we are capable of, of the power of prejudice so easily aroused to fuel hate. But Anne also gives us hope, the hope she had, that all can be well again, if we make it well. Her words, her suffering, her death, give us the determination to right the wrongs of anti-semitism and prejudice of all kinds, to create a world where kindness, empathy and understanding rule.

Because of Anne, scribbling away up in her crowded attic room, I have had her story and her fate, and the iniquitous and vile Holocaust, in my head for much of my life. It's no accident then that I have written my own stories about it.

Growing up, I was unaware of the Jewish origins of my step-family. My birth name is Bridge, my father an actor, Tony Bridge, but my mother left him in 1946 to marry one Jack Morpurgo, from a Jewish family that emigrated to London in the early twentieth century. So, aged two, I became a Morpurgo. It is a Jewish name from northern Italy, well respected there. Many, many Morpurgos, I later discovered, had died in the camps.

And there was the violin. Go to the Violins of Hope Museum in Tel Aviv and you will find amongst all the violins played in the concentration camps the Morpurgo violin. It belonged to one Galtiero Morpurgo, a survivor of the camps, who was still playing the violin until he died aged 97. His family donated his violin to the museum.

THE VIOLIN OF HOPE

Strangely, I did not know about this Morpurgo violin when, 20 years before, I wrote a story I called *The Mozart Question*. It is to me perhaps my most important book. By this time, I had of course read Primo Levi. I had become good friends with Judith Kerr, a fellow children's writer and Jewish author of *When Hitler Stole Pink Rabbit*, based on her family's escape from Germany in 1933.

I had also discovered that a great teacher of mine, Paul Pollock, who had taught me classics at school, had been a child on the last train of Jewish children to leave Nazi-occupied Prague in 1939, one of hundreds saved from the Holocaust by the wonderful Nicholas Winton. Mr Pollock was a devoted and eccentric teacher much respected for his extraordinary intelligence and famous for his withering remarks. His barber was once overheard asking him: 'And how would you like your hair cut today, sir?' 'In silence,' Mr Pollock replied. He died only six months ago, at over a hundred years old. And we never realised when we were boys what he had been through, how he had no family but us. They'd all gone. He was alone in the world.

His story and others connect me to the Holocaust. But Anne Frank was the first and most important of these connections, and she did not survive. But the diary she wrote hiding away in her attic room in Amsterdam is for so many millions around the world the first and most lasting connection to those times, to those lost millions of the Holocaust, each of whom was a living, breathing, precious human being – a daughter, a son, a mother, a father.

It is because of all this, because of them and all they lived through, that I know as we all do that prejudice has to be fought, that it is a disease that can so easily become an epidemic of hate, a pandemic that can overwhelm us if we ignore it or look the other way. We have to be vigilant; this hate has to be confronted. Historical awareness and stories can help in this struggle.

I'm firmly convinced that unless we know and remain aware of where prejudice can and does lead, unless we know the history of the Holocaust, then it can happen again, again and again. And I'm also convinced that it is stories that can keep us vigilant, can make all of us growing up aware, generation after generation.

We owe it to them, to those who died in the Holocaust, to Anne Frank, and to those who survived, to go on telling the story.

And we surely owe it to them to do more, to seek peace and reconciliation, to create the kind of world I discovered on my visit to Israel and Gaza ten or so years ago with Save the Children. Such a place, such a spirit, such children and families, and teachers, will put the world to rights. There was hope there, there was peace there. Hope springs eternal and hope brings peace. Let there be peace.

FINDING ALFIE

2024

There was a time when the books I was writing for young people were often dismissed as nostalgic or irrelevant. Less often now, I hope.

War Horse was one such story. Although it was shortlisted for the Whitbread Prize in 1982, it was the opinion of some of the judges, I was told, that children weren't interested in history, that war was the past. Children liked to live, I was advised, in the now. I'd been a teacher for eight years, and a father too, so I knew this wasn't true. How else can we begin to comprehend today, or conceive of tomorrow, if we know nothing about yesterday?

On the way to school in post-war London, I had to walk past a blind veteran who was often sitting outside the sweet shop playing a mouth organ. He had a Jack Russell that bared its teeth and growled at me, even when I was walking by on the other side of the road. I never liked to go too close to that dog, or the veteran. Others did and would drop coins sometimes into his upturned helmet. He saluted everyone who did.

FINDING ALFIE

I had another reason for not going too near. The blind soldier always dressed smartly and wore a row of medals on his blue blazer with silver buttons. Everything about him was tidy and I liked the tunes he played. But all I could think about was that he had only one leg, one shoe. His other trouser leg was folded underneath him somehow. His missing leg horrified me and haunted me, but also fascinated me. I would dare to stare at him sometimes as I passed by, but my mother's hand would tighten on mine and she would tell me not to stare, that it was rude.

I learnt that same lesson when a family friend came to visit. Eric Pearce was always smart, his shoes shining, and he had a gold watch chain that dangled from his waistcoat pocket. He had been a pilot in the Fleet Air Arm, I'd been told, had won lots of medals and was very brave. He'd spent the war flying his plane from an aircraft carrier out at sea, attacking German submarines.

But I wasn't so interested in that. I was much more fascinated by one side of Eric's face, by his left ear that was hardly there, by his strange wandering eye that didn't seem to see, by the reddened skin that looked unnaturally thin and stretched over his cheekbone, and by his hand with fewer fingers. In the war, my mother told me, Eric's plane had crash landed and burst into flames. He'd been dragged from the burning wreckage badly burnt, nearly dead, and spent years in hospital. I learnt some years later that Eric Pearce had been one of Dr Archibald McIndoe's patients in the pioneering burns unit at Victoria Hospital in East Grinstead.

Every time Eric came to tea, my mother impressed upon me again that it was rude to stare. However hard I tried, though, my eyes seemed to be drawn to his face. I met Eric 60 or more years later, when he was nearly a hundred years old, and apologised for staring at him as I had. He smiled and told me he hadn't minded one bit. He much preferred it when people stared, he told me, than when they looked the other way.

Amongst these childhood heroes too was Ian Macleod, or 'Mac' as we called him, another close family friend. He had served in the Royal Army Medical Corps during the war, and afterwards became the physiotherapist to the MCC at Lords. He collected little autographed cricket bats for me, signed by many of my sporting heroes in the England team – Peter May, Trevor Bailey, Len Hutton and Fred Truman amongst them. Mac was a hero to me for that, and because he made the best gravy in the world, and because he was the kindest man I ever knew.

But Mac was also a hero for another and far more significant reason. In 1945, as a young medical orderly, he had been in the first convoy of ambulances that had driven into the Bergen-Belsen concentration camp when it was liberated by British troops on 15 April 1945 – just two weeks, it is thought, after Anne Frank had died there. Barely more than a teenager at the time, the effect of all he had witnessed there, the suffering of the prisoners, the sick and the starving, and the dying and the dead, was to haunt Mac for the rest of his life. He tended them, comforted them, buried them. He never spoke of it, but others who knew about it did. As I grew up, I realised that it was his time as a soldier at Bergen-Belsen that was destroying him slowly in front of our eyes.

My uncle Pieter was simply a photograph on the mantelpiece at home when I was growing up. He was the uncle I never met. All I knew was that my mother, his sister, who adored him, often cried when anyone mentioned his name.

He was in the RAF, in Bomber Command, based in Cornwall. He had been on a raid over German-occupied France. But his plane had been hit over their target in Brest and the pilot was too badly hurt to go on flying it. My uncle Pieter was a sergeant navigator – he had never flown a plane before. As they came in over the coast of Cornwall, Pieter flying the plane as best he could, he told the rest of the crew to bale out. Knowing the pilot was too badly injured to jump, he tried to land the plane himself at his home base at St Eval.

FUNNY THING, GETTING OLDER

The plane crashed on landing and they were both killed. The remainder of the crew lived.

Uncle Pieter was 22 when he died. He had been an actor, trained at RADA, and was extraordinarily handsome in his photograph. He is buried in the churchyard in Radlett, near his parents' home. His courage has inspired me all my life.

The story of Uncle Pieter's elder brother, Francis Cammaerts, has been just as influential. Uncle Francis was a teacher. He was also a socialist and a pacifist. So when war was declared, he took a very different path from Uncle Pieter, who had joined up almost at once. Francis had to go before a tribunal to convince them his pacifism was genuine. He was sent to help on a farm in Lincolnshire, ploughing and sowing, shepherding sheep, raising pigs.

Then he heard that his beloved brother had been killed. Unwilling now to stay out of it, he joined up. A teacher friend of his, Harry Ree, had joined some mysterious unit he said he could not talk about and advised Francis to go along to see them. That Francis spoke fluent French would help, he said. So Francis went along to an address in London that Harry gave him and within a few months found himself being trained up in Scotland, as a secret agent in the Special Operations Executive, and then dropped into France to link up with the Resistance there. In two years, he effectively became the leader of 10,000 Maquis Resistance fighters across the whole south of France. He was known to be brave as a lion, never rash, a formidable organiser and much loved by all who fought with him. He soon had a price on his head, sought after by the Gestapo and the Milice – the French police collaborating with the occupiers.

One rare mistake at a checkpoint in the last weeks before the Americans landed to liberate the south of France saw him and his companions arrested, interrogated, locked up in the Gestapo headquarters in Digne and awaiting execution the following morning. He was saved only because his closest colleague and dear friend, the Polish agent Christine Granville, who had heard about his arrest, brazenly walked into the Gestapo headquarters in Digne and told the officer in charge that she was a British agent, related to Field Marshal Montgomery – she spun a good yarn! – and that she knew they were holding Roger, her 'husband', Francis Cammaerts and fellow Resistance fighters in prison there, and that unless they were released unharmed, either the Americans when they landed or the French Resistance would exact a most unpleasant and dire punishment on him.

The officer demanded money, a large sum of money. Christine said she would get it, the deal was done and she left, her warning ringing in the man's head as to what would happen to him if he reneged on the deal. She returned 48 hours later, paid the money which had been flown in from London and they all drove away to freedom.

After the war, Francis went straight back to teaching. I was fortunate to get to know him well in his old age.

After school, I found myself wondering what path in life to take. I think I wanted to prove myself in the same fire in which both my uncles had been tested. I joined up, became a soldier, went to Sandhurst, learnt more about comradeship, less about shooting straight or polishing boots perfectly. I left the army and went off to university, then into teaching, and through teaching into writing.

But it's hardly surprising that war, and the terrible consequences of it, have played such a prominent part in my stories over the years.

There is a difficulty in writing about the suffering of war, when I know my readers are often very young. The principle underlying all my books is one I learnt as a teacher. Very early on, when I was finding my voice as a storyteller in the classroom of Wickhambreaux Primary School, I would use the last half hour of every day to tell my Year 6 class a story – either one of my own or an adaptation of some folk tale. I discovered quickly that if I wanted to keep their attention I had to mean the story, believe it and live it as I told it – and

FINDING ALFIE

look them in the eye. Above all, I knew that I must not ever patronise them.

As a teacher and a parent, I did not want my stories to traumatise. But to see children saddened, deep in thought, working out the rights and wrongs, the fair and the unfair, was important. Many would have known grief already. Some would have serious difficulties at home. I felt that the stories I was telling should not avoid the painful side of life.

War is part of the world into which they have been born. They know this all too well, and all too soon in their young lives, that's for sure. The children of today come across images of war on their phones: of bombs falling, of whole towns destroyed before their eyes. They see unimaginable scenes of suffering in hospitals under siege. They witness families grieving over dead bodies. They hear and see stories, vividly told, of the consequences of war, too: the starvation, the disease, the drowning of migrants escaping conflict. I'm sure the instinct often is to switch off, or to look away, but once seen, such images are difficult to forget, and they can be deeply troubling to the young mind. But the young mind is endlessly inquisitive. Children want to know, to discover more of the unknown, even if it is disturbing.

I have tried never to shy away from writing stories about those moments in history or in my life that have affected me deeply. A visit to Venice gave me cause to write a story, for instance, about the Holocaust. One night, walking over the Accademia Bridge, we came down into a piazza and witnessed the sublime – a street violinist playing the most exquisite music: Mozart. Then we saw a young boy of four or five sitting some distance away on his tricycle in his pyjamas totally lost in the music. We stayed, not wanting the moment to end.

The next day, we walked down an alleyway into the Jewish quarter, from which, we discovered, more than 200 Jews had been deported to concentration camps in 1944. Very few returned. Heaven on earth it had been the night before, listening with the boy to the violinist playing Mozart. Now here was a reminder of hell on earth.

I wrote *The Mozart Question* shortly after, my story of the power of music over evil. Yes, it's about the horror of the camps, but it's also about the survivors, how they and their descendants deal with the enormity of the loss, and how music enriches their lives.

The generation before us did not look the other way. Eighty years ago, Allied troops set out from the shores of Britain in the biggest seaborne invasion ever made to liberate occupied Europe. At dawn on 6 June, they began their landings on the beaches of Normandy. Many died on those beaches, but there was no shaking the resolve of our forefathers. They never surrendered, they fought on the beaches, and within a year, they had defeated perhaps the worst tyranny that ever threatened mankind.

Those beaches were not far from Dunkirk, where, four years before, more than 300,000 soldiers had been picked up by the Royal Navy and that famous armada of little boats and brought back to safety. A defeated army lived to fight on again another day. And that day was D-Day.

My book *Finding Alfie* is a story of one of those brave soldiers who was there at Dunkirk in one of the little boats to help bring the army home and, four years later, was there at the Normandy landings.

Wilfred Owen once wrote of 'the pity of war'. It is that pity I write about. That's what I want to pass on to my readers, adult or child, wherever they live. I like to think of my stories as reminders of how the past was for those who lived it, ever hopeful for a brighter future, ever more sure that freedom is worth defending, and that we should never take it for granted.

A STRANGE MEETING IN AN OXFORD RESTAURANT

2024

One evening, after some literary event in Oxford, we were out having a quiet meal. Not the best meal. I'd talked at the event and I was feeling relieved that a few people had turned up, and that it had gone well enough. We had finished eating when a man approached our table. He was tentative and rather apologetic. He was tall and getting on in years, but looked enormously distinguished. He had a face I thought I knew.

'My wife and I were at your talk this evening,' he said. 'I just wanted to say how much we enjoyed it. I hope you don't mind my disturbing you.' He held out his hand. 'My name's Roger Bannister,' he said.

Celebrities there were none, not as we know them today. There were football stars of course – I collected them on Turf cigarette cards. Stanley Mathews, Billy Wright and the like.

But when I was eight or nine, around the time of the late Queen's coronation, there was a glowing time of heroes –

A STRANGE MEETING IN AN OXFORD RESTAURANT

universally admired heroes who seemed to define the postwar optimism of the new Elizabethan age. We'd had the Festival of Britain in 1951. The new young Queen was crowned in 1953. On almost the same day, Tenzing Norgay and Edmund Hillary summitted Everest, the first mountaineers to do so. And in 1951, in Oxford, on the university running track, a medical student became the first athlete in the world to run a mile in under four minutes.

The news of these great happenings was beamed around the country and around the world on newsreel films, to early television sets. These were my three towering examples of achievement and endurance: two of them standing at the top of the world after their record-breaking climb, and one breasting the tape exhausted after running a mile faster than anyone else had ever done.

And there I was meeting one of them in a fish restaurant in Oxford, a 60-year-old writer struggling for words in front of the great Roger Bannister. I knew by now that he had been not just one of the greatest athletes the world had ever known, but had devoted his working life to medicine, to the lives of others. As indeed had Tenzing and Hillary.

Roger Bannister joined us at our table with his wife, and we talked and talked. We met up with them and their family again the next time we went to Oxford. He was in a wheelchair by this time and not well. What I recall about him was his modesty, and his kind and generous spirit. He was a true hero, untainted by his fame or fortune. He wore it lightly and used it – if he did at all – never for self- glorification nor to make a fortune, but to serve people, care for them, cure them.

We are soon to be launched into the feverish hype of the next Olympic Games, in Paris. It was, of course, a Frenchman, the Baron Pierre de Coubertin, who was largely responsible for resuscitating the Olympic Games in the modern era in the 1890s, which the Ancient Greeks had invented in the eighth century BC. At about the same time as Coubertin in France was struggling to bring to fruition his dream of creating a new Olympic era, in Much Wenlock, a small village in Gloucestershire, one Dr Brookes, inspired by the philosophy of Thomas Arnold of Rugby School, was already pioneering his own, more local version of the Olympics. Coubertin came to have a look and was in his turn inspired to go further.

Both pioneers had similar founding principles at heart: to enable young people to engage in sports, to give them a greater sense of purpose and fulfilment, and most importantly, to bring people and communities together. Coubertin, much affected by having witnessed the destruction of war, saw the Olympic ideal as a powerful way to

A STRANGE MEETING IN AN OXFORD RESTAURANT

bring nations together, to create lasting peace. These noble and ambitious notions had their roots of course in the Ancient Greek Games. It may be that their take on the original Olympics was rather overly idealistic. That's still up for debate. It took decades for Coubertin, a passionate educationist first and foremost, to persuade the world that his dream should become a reality. He wanted the first restored Olympics to take place in Paris, but the Greeks and others decided in the end on Athens as the location for the 1896 Games. The Olympics were coming home. Paris had to wait until 1900.

Meanwhile, the people of Much Wenlock, inspired by Dr Brookes, quietly went on holding their modest mini Olympics every year, engaging ever-more widespread communities, with more and more people taking part. Between these two differing but unifying movements, the spirit of the ancient Olympics was slowly reemerging – yet it was into a world where war was threatening, particularly in Europe. To the founders and supporters everywhere, it was obvious the Games were needed even more urgently. We know that again today, in our increasingly confrontational world.

One world war later, in 1924, a hundred years ago, the Olympic Games were back in Paris. We know these Games rather better than others because of the film, of course –

FUNNY THING, GETTING OLDER

Chariots of Fire. The stadium was smaller in 1924; there were far fewer athletes, events, flags, participating nations. Not so many national anthems were sung and there was much less hype than there is today, too. But after that war, the need was clearly understood. The Olympic Games were about training hard, doing your best and winning, yes, but they were also about peace, about enabling peoples of countries far and wide, competitors and supporters, to come together and make common cause of mutual understanding and peace.

At the heart of the British team in these Paris Games of 1924, there was, famously, a remarkable Scotsman, Eric Liddell, who refused on religious grounds to run his race on a Sunday, his day of worship. Common sense prevailed and he was permitted to change his event to the 400 metres, run on another day, in which he won a gold medal anyway. He was amateur, they were all amateur. Which necessarily meant that an athlete could not earn a living from running or any kind of athletics. Sports was more often than not a preserve of those who could afford it. Wonderfully, sport, from horseriding to swimming to the marathon, is now much more open to all. It is a recognised pathway in schools through which young people can develop a healthy lifestyle, in body and mind.

A STRANGE MEETING IN AN OXFORD RESTAURANT

The notion that sport is for all, because it is of benefit to all, was further broadened by Ludwig Guttmann in 1944. A doctor at Stoke Mandeville Hospital for wounded Second World War veterans, Guttmann wanted to encourage his patients to rediscover their mental and physical health through sport – specifically, archery to start with. Guttmann's initiative led in time to a worldwide movement that has now developed to become a parallel Olympic Games, the Paralympics.

Given the right opportunity and encouragement, the teachers and coaches, the playing fields and facilities, there is these days far wider access to participation in sport of all kinds, for all kinds of people too. Provision is far from even or enough across society, but how Coubertin and the pioneers of Much Wenlock would have loved to see the progress that has been made educationally. And they would have admired also the pleasure so many of us derive from sport as spectators, and as recreation to be enjoyed by billions across the world.

But those great pioneers would be able to see that, despite such extraordinary progress, all is far from well as we come towards the Olympic Games in France this summer. There is the inexorable rise of the power of money and of nationalism in sport, and a culture where winning is everything. It can be a toxic combination. We know that in the decades of the Cold War, nations like East Germany and others contrived to raise the prestige of their state and its system by training and indoctrinating young athletes that they must win at all costs, by any means, using drugs if necessary. And yet, before we point fingers too much, there is for me a question mark over any state support in sports. We do it now in Britain, as do most countries. The culture is to support mostly those sports where we win. We like to see our flag go up, like to see ourselves high up the medal table. Nationalism in excess, like money in excess, is contrary to the Olympic ideal.

A recent threat to the integrity of the Olympic Games is the payment of £50,000 proposed for some gold medal winners. Is not winning the medal enough, for your country, for your team? Why must money come into this? Did not the one who came fourth or last try as hard as the winner? Is winning everything? By all means pay our athletes, pay them properly, it's their profession, they deserve it. But do we want them to be superstar multimillionaire celebrities or heroes that we can look up to and admire? I prefer the latter.

I never discussed all this with Roger Bannister. I wish I had. He too wanted to win, that's for sure. But I like to think and believe that he would have told me that it really was the

A STRANGE MEETING IN AN OXFORD RESTAURANT

taking part, the achievement and the mastery of skill, the sheer joy of running and winning, and the companionship of fellow athletes, friends, that was important. It was not the money, not the celebrity he ran for. He ran only to achieve the best he could.

Ask children today, as I often have, what they want in life, and an all-too frequent and depressing response might be money or fame, or both. This is hardly surprising. From early years, they are inculcated with the notion that nothing is more important, more admired in society at large. The baubles of wealth and celebrity are dangled in front of them. Not surprising, then, that many reach out for them. Footballers, for instance, are often judged as much by the fortune they can earn as by how they play or the goals they score or save.

There are those, across all sport, including great footballers such as Marcus Rashford, who rise above that; many athletes who clearly want to give back to society more than they take, like Roger Bannister. They earn our admiration and respect. They are the worthy heroes. And there are many of them in sport.

I should like to think that the Olympics will uphold the spirit that has sustained the Games for centuries, that the glory is in the laurel wreath or the medal, not the money rewards, that it is the taking part that is heroic, the triumphs and the disappointments. My wife had a relation, Ngaire Lane, who came to the London Olympics in 1948 to swim for New Zealand. He came near to last. There is much heroism in that.

The Olympics these days might have to have the hype, the prestige and all the razzmatazz. I prefer my razzmatazz, if I'm honest, to involve a bear having tea with a queen. They can't do that in France but they can swim in the Seine, which must be cleaner than our Thames, and that's wonderful. And along with little Much Wenlock, the French did reinvent it. So bravo Baron Coubertin, bravo Dr Brooke, bravo Ludwig Guttmann. *Vive La France*, and *Vive Les Jeux Olympiques*, *Vive Les Jeux Paralympiques*!

And bravo, especially, to the great and the good Roger Bannister.

TELLING TALES

WILL THERE BE SINGING?

2023

Speech for a conference on education.

Bertolt Brecht once asked: 'In the dark times, will there be singing?'

I will answer that later.

The concern I have is that I know and you know that I am talking to the essentially like-minded. We may differ – but even then perhaps only minimally – as to how we achieve what we are all hoping for, seeking and working for: a culture in which to love and cherish books, creativity and reading is common to everyone; a society in which literature is universally valued and respected, felt to belong to us all, helping us to grow intellectually and emotionally, uniting us; a society where homes and schools encourage children to grow up listening to and reading stories, where the school library is thought of as the cultural centre of every school and community. Get all that right and we are a long way to becoming an educated people. We all want that. Our fragile democracy needs that.

FUNNY THING, GETTING OLDER

We know, without reminding ourselves endlessly, the obvious and less obvious benefits children can glean from developing a lifelong love of reading – the widening and deepening of knowledge and understanding; the ability to empathise, to explore and discover; to be comforted, excited, provoked and challenged; the spur to confidence and creativity.

Like many wordsmiths and storymakers, I speak of all this often, rather too often, I fear. At conferences here and there, at literary festivals, at gatherings of likeminded folk. Our hope of course when we do this is that we provoke debate, that this debate will help to change attitudes and ultimately contribute to the enriching of children's lives, and life chances, through a love of stories. That's my hope.

But is this a vain hope? What are we doing this for? What is the point? Who will be listening, except ourselves? I, like many, can sing the old song; blow the trumpet, bang the drum for the love of books, the importance of literacy for our children. I proclaim it loud. I can bemoan the closing of libraries, the homes where parents don't read to their children, the schools where stories and poems can still so often be used simply as fodder for teaching literacy to the test.

I could blame successive governments and education ministers who have indulged in short-termism in their education policies, who corral schools and pressure teachers – yes, often through the demands of Ofsted – into teaching literacy fearfully, who insist that measurable outcomes and results are the be all and end all of the education process, who often make a chore and a trial out of reading and books, who have succeeded so often only in banishing the enjoyment of reading for pleasure.

But that would be passing the buck. Their fault, not ours. Wrong. We live in a democracy – just. An imperfect democracy, certainly. Indeed, books and literature have played a crucial role over the centuries in creating and preserving our democratic system as well as the freedoms and rights we now so often take for granted – the freedom to speak our mind, our freedom to choose what we read and write. We choose our governments. We are all of us in some way responsible both for the successes and failures of our literacy and our society, for they are, as we know, intimately connected. So when it comes to reading and books, if we have failed to engage and enthuse generations of children, especially those millions from less advantaged backgrounds – and most certainly we have failed far too many of them – then for all of us, amongst so many of us who have striven to create a more literate society, it is *mea culpa, mea maxima culpa*.

Indeed, I think it could and should be said that literacy, or the lack of it, divides us, fractures our wider community. It

FUNNY THING, GETTING OLDER

helps define and separate those who have from those who have not, those who feel they belong and those who feel they do not, those who feel empowered and those who feel they are not, those who feel alienated. The truth is that over the years, the centuries, reading and literacy amongst our children, in our society, has certainly grown but sadly it is also true it has not been all inclusive, as it should have been. Far from it. And that has been the great failure on our part.

But let me focus a while on the positive, on the progress that has been made and what has been achieved by so many people, and not just in our time but over the centuries before us. We should see this progress in some kind of historical perspective, to see where we are, where we have come from and what still remains to be done.

This striving for a society which encourages reading and writing, where knowledge and understanding are accepted as important, indeed vital, to our wellbeing as well as our productivity, our cohesion as a tribe, our sense of belonging – all this striving was not entirely down to King Alfred. But I like to think he helped begin it. I like Good King Alfred, Alfred the Great, because I love a good story. I am one of those sleepy heads inclined to let the toast burn at breakfast, so I feel for the man. He was tired, for goodness sakes, exhausted by his efforts to drive out the dastardly Danes, but not too tired once he had done it to put his mind to the education of the people. He knew education and reading were the way forward. He pointed the way. So thanks for that, Good King Alfred.

The church then held the baton of education and reading and writing for many centuries – I myself went to a school founded by St Augustine. Seventh century, so quite old. But then I was at school a long time ago! So thanks for that, St Augustine. All right, so there was another agenda here. In reading terms, it is true there was predominantly only one bestseller out there, the Bible – a book, by the way, that is a treasure trove of great stories. But the growth of those early schools and universities slowly spread the notion, through the monks, to the people. The understanding grew that this world of reading was beneficial both to our prospects in this world and the next, to our growth of knowledge and spiritual wellbeing. The notion developed amongst the people that words were power, that we could use them to search for truth, to have our say. There was a growing thirst for written law and written rights. The written word mattered, framed laws, framed Magna Carta.

And all the while, let us not forget, the old stories were being told aloud, passed around, passed on, sometimes sung and performed in town squares or village greens – ancient stories from earlier times that had their origins in myths and legends of our own and from far away too, brought to us from the distant lands of traders, travellers and invaders. We have always had our stories and our songs, renewed and retold for each generation. They helped make us who we have become, to find out about other peoples, other cultures, and to keep us in touch with who we have been.

Then technology gave us all in this country a huge helping hand, truly a giant leap for man and womankind, childkind as well. William Caxton thought up the printing press. Now, stories and poems and pamphlets could be printed in their dozens, and then in hundreds and thousands. No longer did everything have to be copied out laboriously, and often beautifully, exquisitely, by monks. No longer could the church hold such sway over what we wrote and read. The book genie, the story genie, the knowledge genie – call it what you will – was well and truly out of the bottle.

The book took off, went viral. So thanks for that, Mr Caxton! What an invention, Mr Caxton! Still going strong, more needed that ever! The printed word could now be read by anyone who could read, and because of the printing press more and more people could read, and more and more people wanted to read. This reading thing was spreading like wildfire. Knowledge was for everyone. Stories and ideas were for everyone. To feed this yearning for stories, ever more poems and plays were written and performed. Theatres sprang up. Shakespeare happened. And from where did he discover the plots for so many of his plays? From the stories he read and he grew up with, that had been passed down to him, that he learnt at school, from books, from history.

The book, the play, was new and exciting, but seriously dangerous to those who wished to control the way we thought. This spread of new ideas through reading and performing was overturning old, dried-up myths, revolutionising our thinking, opening up new possibilities, new concepts, new scientific discovery, raising hopes and aspirations. The people were finding out that any emperor's new clothes were somewhat transparent, even non-existent! The world was round. God did not bestow divine right on kings and he would have found it impossible to create the world in seven days. Darwin ensured, in his *The Origin of Species*, that other ideas as to how we had evolved as a species were discussed. They seemed to make more sense.

The more we read, the more we realised that we had the right to life, liberty and the pursuit of happiness; the right to speak our minds, express our ideas; the right to strive for greater freedom, fairness and equality. We realised we needed books to expand our horizons, to make sense of this often dark and difficult world, as well as of ourselves and our lives on this beautiful, tormented and fragile planet. Make no mistake – it was not simply strife and struggle that achieved all this: it was the written word, the printed word, the book, and the courage of women and men, who so often risked life and limb to write.

Yet even at the beginning of the twentieth century, after all this time, there were still millions mired in poverty, hunger and illiteracy, effectively alienated and disenfranchised. Despite the spread of education, despite the new libraries being built in towns and cities up and down the country, there were still those children who could not read, who had scarcely ever seen a book, never had one in the house. Books were expensive to buy. A good education was by no means universally available and sometimes too minimal to make much difference to the lives people could lead, to their prospects. The elite had to a large extent taken possession of this new world of the written word, seeming to want to keep it exclusive, expensive, to manipulate it for their own purposes. For so many, this new world of knowledge and understanding was still tragically unattainable.

But books and education, and the ideas they had sown and nurtured, would not be denied. In this country in the 1930s, little orange paperback books appeared on our

WILL THERE BE SINGING?

bookstalls, with a jovial little penguin dancing on the front covers. They were cheap, sixpence a copy. Now books became rampant. So, thank you, Mr Penguin. These were books for everyone – and all sorts of books too: crime, mystery, poetry, great classics from all over the world. Books you could slip into your pocket, take anywhere, read anywhere. Books were not exclusive any more. Books were on a roll. Good books too.

There was the BBC now broadcasting into millions of homes – so thank you, Mr BBC, Mr Reith – books being read out, stories new and old, dramatised. There was poetry too and even some programmes for children. Out of the horrors of war, and the burning pyres of books, came a peace built on hope, and on a determination to extend rights and power to everyone, through education, through knowledge and ideas. There were ever more libraries and bookshops. The 1944 Education Act ensured a better education for our young. More and more publishers were bringing out children's books – all sorts and kinds, fiction and non-fiction – and more and more people were reading them, writing them and illustrating them, and telling them and selling them. For children, for all of us, it really was going to be the best of all possible worlds. Now we were all of us, irrespective of income, geography or background, going to be able to enjoy the benefits of reading, and through books to be more able to follow a pathway to fulfilment.

I was reading these books – not often enough, I was told – and comics too, and listening to children's radio, from about 1948. But there was no library at St Matthias, my Church of England, London County Council school on the Warwick Road in west London, no books for enjoyment, just school textbooks, readers. I had loved stories before I went to that school because my mother read to us, only her favourite stories and poems. She read them with a passion. My brother and I loved them with a passion. They were fun, they were exciting; l longed for storytime. It was our time alone with her, just her, the three of us and the story we were living together as she read.

School killed all that, took the wonder of stories, the music and playfulness of language, and turned it all into a 'subject' to be used for comprehension tests, handwriting tests, grammar tests, parsing, spelling tests and punctuation tests. In these tests, at least as many of us failed as succeeded. Testing is supposed to encourage both. It doesn't. When you fail, it brings only a sense of worthlessness and hopelessness. It brings fear, shame and anxiety. It separates you from those who have passed, rocks confidence, ruins self-esteem. You disappoint yourself, disappoint others. You give up. I gave up.

WILL THERE BE SINGING?

To give up on books is to give up on education, and if you give up on education then you can so easily give up on hope, give up on your future. This way, you can so easily turn children away from books and reading, and that can be a life sentence, a life without books. So many avenues are barred, so many possibilities never imagined, so many discoveries never made, so much understanding of yourself, of others, stunted for ever.

But I was lucky. I was granted a second chance. I had a mother who had sowed the seed early on, passed on to me her love of words and stories and poems. I had enough wonderful and inspiring teachers in each of my three schools, and then at university, to begin to restore my confidence. They helped grow the seed which had almost died in me. I was fortunate indeed. I was later to become a teacher and in a sense, I have never in my adult life not been a teacher.

Yet, despite my best efforts as a teacher, and the best efforts before me of King Alfred, William Caxton, William Shakespeare, libraries, paperback books, publishers, great writers and illustrators, and thousands upon thousands of talented teachers and devoted parents, there still exists almost an apartheid system of a kind in this country, between have and have-not children, between those who read, who through books, through developing an enjoyment of literature, can have the opportunity to access the considerable cultural and material benefits of our society; and those who were made to feel very early on that the world of words, of books, of stories, of ideas, is not for them – that they are not clever enough to join that world, that it is not one they can belong to. It may then be shut off from them for ever. In the country of Shakespeare, Wordsworth and Hughes, and of Dahl, Pullman and Rowling, the great divide is still there. Shamefully still there. Alfred the Great's dream is still not fulfilled.

I may, I hope, have helped some of the children I taught on their way. I may have, through my storymaking, encouraged some children to become readers for life. But not enough, not enough. There are far too many children I failed – as a teacher, and as a writer and campaigner too. Our prisons are full of those we have failed. Many remain lonely and marginalised all their lives. The right book, the right author, the right parent, the right teacher, the right librarian at the right time might have saved some of them at least, made the difference, shone a light into a dark life, turned that life around. So, in spite of our best intentions – of politicians, yes, and writers, illustrators, storytellers, the whole publishing and bookselling world, libraries, theatres, parents, all of us – to reach out and include, millions of our children still feel excluded and alienated. What are we to do? Where have we gone wrong?

Well, it's obvious. Let me be quite explicit about this, just in case I haven't been already. It's the story, stupid! The story! We know what works and it really is simple. Mum and Dad telling stories, reading stories they love too; teachers given the time and space within every school day – 3 p.m. to 3.30 p.m. is best – to do the same; a good library in every school and in the community; writers, storytellers and illustrators visiting schools, telling their tales, drawing their pictures, singing their songs; theatres reaching out to family audiences and coming into schools with their productions, as many do, shows being put on at prices families can afford.

So what more can we do? Most certainly, we have to go on singing the song, blowing the trumpet, banging the drum. But just talking about it, writing about it, giving lectures about it amongst ourselves certainly doesn't put it right. There must be a realisation that all that matters at an early age is that children learn to love the story, that they want to listen to more, read them, tell them, write them, act them out, sing them, dance them. All the rest will come later – the literacy side of things, which is important, once that seed is sown. Sow seed on stony ground, try to make it grow with no sun and no rain, and it won't happen. You cannot force-feed children with literacy. Metaphors are better mixed! Punctuation lessons never inspired reading for pleasure, nor did grammar of any kind, nor did testing. Encourage parents, unchain the teachers, take away the fear. Children have to want to learn. So give them the love of story first and the rest will follow. Horse before cart, horse before cart.

All of us who live in this world of making books or loving books need no reminding of the power of books to transform the lives of children, to release their creative energy and genius. We do not need convincing of this. But I can, I hope, try to remind us of the power of stories for all of us, child or grown-up child, by reading a story. So, to finish, a story about storytelling.

I began with Bertolt Brecht, if you remember, and a question. Let's end with an answer, my answer.

'In the dark times, will there be singing?' he asks.

'Yes, Mr Brecht,' I tell him. 'There will be singing, and storytelling and reading too, and writing maybe, Mr Brecht. That's maybe the only way we can come one day out of the darkness and into the light, the light of knowledge and understanding.'

Here is a part of one of my books:

WILL THERE BE SINGING?

I Believe in Unicorns
One afternoon the unicorn lady took out from her bag a rather old and damaged looking book, all charred at the edges. It was, she told us, her very own copy of The Little Match Girl *by Hans Christian Andersen. I was sitting that day very close to the unicorn lady's feet, looking up at the book. 'Why's it been burnt?' I asked her.*

This is the most precious book I have, Tomas, she said. 'I'll tell you why. When I was very little I lived in another country. There were wicked people in my town who were frightened of the magic of stories and of the power of books, because stories make you think and dream; books make you want to ask questions. And they didn't want that. I was there with my father watching them burn a great pile of books, when suddenly my father ran forward and plucked a book out of the fire. The soldiers beat him with sticks, but he held on to the book and wouldn't let go of it. It was this book. It's my favourite book in all the world. Tomas, would you like to come and sit on the unicorn and read it to us?'

I had never been any good at reading out loud. I would always stutter over my consonants, worry over long words. But now, sitting on the magic unicorn, I heard my voice strong and loud. It was like singing a song. The words danced on the air and everyone listened. That same day I took home

FUNNY THING, GETTING OLDER

my first book from the library, Aesop's fables, because the unicorn lady had read them to us and I'd loved them. I read them aloud to my mother that night, the first time I'd ever read to her, and I could see she was amazed. I loved amazing my mother.

Then one summer morning, early, war came to our valley and shattered our lives. Before that morning I knew little of war. I knew some of the men had gone to fight, but I wasn't sure what for. I had seen on television tanks shooting at houses and soldiers with guns running through the trees, but my mother always told me it was far away and I wasn't to worry.

I remember that moment. I was outside. My mother had sent me out to open up the hens and feed them, when I looked up and saw a single plane come flying in low over the town. I watched as it circled once and came away again. That was when the bombs began to fall, far away at first, then closer, closer. We were all running then, running up into the woods. I was too frightened to cry. My father cried. I'd never seen him cry before, but it was from anger as much as fear.

Hidden in the woods we could see the tans and the soldiers all over the town, blasting and shooting as they went. A few hours later, after they had gone, we could hardly see the town

WILL THERE BE SINGING?

any more for the smoke. We waited until we were quite sure they had all gone, and then we ran back home. We were luckier than many. Our house had not been damaged. It was soon obvious that the centre of town had been hardest hit. Everyone seemed to be making their way there. I ran on ahead hoping and praying that the library had not been bombed, that the unicorn lady and the unicorn were safe.

As I came into the square I saw smoke rising from the roof of the library and flames licking out of the upper windows. We all saw the unicorn lady at the same moment. She was coming out of the library carrying the unicorn, staggering under its weight. Her eyes were red from the smoke. Between us we set the unicorn down at the foot of the steps, and she sat down exhausted, racked with a fit of coughing. My mother fetched her a glass of water. It must have helped because the coughing stopped, and all at once she was up on her feet, leaning on my shoulder for support.

'The books,' she breathed, 'the books.'

When she began to walk back up the steps I followed her without thinking.

'No, Tomas,' she said. 'You stay here and look after the unicorn.' Then she was running up the steps into the library, only to reappear moments later, her arms piled high with books. That was the moment the rescue began. People

FUNNY THING, GETTING OLDER

seemed suddenly to surge past me up the steps, and into the library, my mother and father among them.

It wasn't long before a whole system was set up. We children made two chains across the square from the library to the café opposite, and the books everyone rescued went from hand to hand, ending up in stacks on the floor of the café. The fire was burning ever more fiercely, the flames crackling, smoke billowing now from the roof. No fire engines came – we found out later the fire station had been hit. Still the books came out. Still the fire burned and more and more people came to help, until the café was filled with books and we had to use the grocer's shop next door.[6]

PERCHANCE TO DREAM

2025

I grew up with King Arthur and his knights, Robin Hood and his band of Merry Men. As a storymaker, I have adapted many ancient myths and legends. It find it wonderful to return to these ancient tales I know so well and retell them for the young of today. In the same way an artist can learn from copying the works of great painters, so I learn from these stories which have endured and been passed on for thousands of years. And, more than once, I, like so many writers and others, have been inspired to visit the places where these ancient stories happened. I have travelled the world in my stories, discovering places and peoples, their tales and their histories. I collect storythread from all over, weave it on my loom and pass it on to young readers.

I have two true stories to tell you. The first is set in these islands. I went on a search for King Arthur. Like the great poet Alfred Lord Tennyson before me, I was writing about King Arthur. It wasn't on a whim. I never write on a whim! Who am I kidding?

FUNNY THING, GETTING OLDER

Here goes. I go to Bryher on the Scilly Isles for my holidays, every year if I can. One summer, I arrived and went as usual to buy our vegetables at the farmer's stall just down the lane from where we were staying. I was just choosing some new potatoes when he came out and invited me in. He had something to show me, he said. And he seemed quite excited. He took me into his greenhouse. On his worktable there lay something covered with a sack.

He didn't immediately show me what it was. Instead, he told me about it. 'I was driving along in my tractor the other day, ploughing, when I suddenly felt my back wheel get stuck in a hole. I got out, looked down and there was this lying there at the bottom.' He pulled back the sack.

It was an ancient sword, rusty but complete, and with it what looked like a mirror and some remains of a cloak. He told me archaeologists had been to look and thought he must have driven into a grave perhaps 2–3,000 years old, that these might be the grave goods, the remains of some ancient chieftain, maybe of around King Arthur's time.

So I'd come to buy potatoes and discovered quite by chance a possible link to one of my childhood heroes, King Arthur. I knew at once I was going to write about this sword and how it came to be there. To me, this was at once Excalibur, King Arthur's sword that he pulled out of the

PERCHANCE TO DREAM

stone, the very sword that his faithful knight, Sir Bedivere, had refused time and again to throw into the lake after the wounded old King's last battle. Although he told the dying king that he had, he never did. In my book, in my story, he kept it. In my mind, this sword had to be Excalibur and the farmer had driven his tractor over Sir Bedivere's tomb. No question about it. I was remaking the legend.

Then I remembered something. On the wall of a hotel on St Mary's, there is a plaque stating that Alfred Lord Tennyson had come to Scilly and stayed there when he was researching the whereabouts of King Arthur's grave. He was in the process of seeking inspiration for his Arthurian poems, way back in the nineteenth century. He knew, as I knew, as many of you might know, that after the last battle – in which his own son, Mordred, had betrayed him – the old King, dying from his wounds, was borne away to a beach in south Cornwall, near the battlefield. There, he was placed on a burial barge by several queens dressed all in black. No one ever discovered where that barge went, where he was laid to rest. Tennyson thought it had to be on the Scilly Isles, which are only 25 miles across the Atlantic from the beach. He came to find out where that barge, where those queens all in black, had taken him. He never found out. I did. I got lucky.

FUNNY THING, GETTING OLDER

I also got scientific. I had a map of the islands. I spread it out on the bed in our room and tried to work out, or guess, to which of the hundred and more little islands King Arthur had been taken. Silly, I know. I ended up closing my eyes, my blind finger circling around, letting Lady Luck dictate where it should land. I opened my eyes. The tip of my finger was right on a tiny island called Little Arthur. True. Promise.

I went out there the next day in a boat, to Little Arthur on the Eastern Isles. There, I found a small beach where a boat or a barge could beach easily, and beyond it we could see a deep, dark cave. That was enough for me. Arthur was there, I was sure of it. In the legend, as you know, he never did die. He is waiting there to this day on Little Arthur, ready to come back as our king when we need him. And do we need him now!

Legends live on, if you retell them. I sat down and wrote my book. I called it *The Sleeping Sword*. Read it if you can and read Tennyson's Arthurian poems too. They're not bad! But don't forget, I was the one who found where Arthur is resting.

I told you there was a second true story, and it's even better. So good you won't believe it.

I had grown up, as many of us have, with that most well-known tale of Ancient Greece, the Trojan Wars, of the great heroes who fought in the years-long siege of the city of Troy, of Odysseus and Achilles, King Menelaus, Hector and King

PERCHANCE TO DREAM

Priam, and of Helen and Paris, who had been the cause of the whole terrible tragedy.

And most memorable of all of course is that great wooden horse, which the Greeks left behind as a gift on the beach, as they apparently gave up, abandoned the siege and sailed away home. We know all too well how the Trojans, rejoicing in their supposed victory, were deluded and deceived, how they brought this wooden horse in through the gates of the city, and how the Greek soldiers hidden inside crept out in the dead of night and opened the gates to let the Greek army in to massacre the Trojans in their sleep.

It was that supreme chronicler of Greek legend, Homer, who told the whole epic story in *The Odyssey*. Homer lived on the island of Ithaca. This was the home also of one of the great heroes of the Trojan Wars, Odysseus. He had left his wife, Penelope, to go to the wars. He was gone ten years, and they were ten years of heroic and fantastical adventures, before he reached home at last after the war was over.

Meanwhile, Penelope, hoping, longing for his return, had been fending off pestering suitors by telling them that she would make up her mind which one of them she would choose only when she had finished her weaving, which she never did finish because every night she unpicked the work she had done in the day.

FUNNY THING, GETTING OLDER

Then one day Odysseus did come home. Let's just say it didn't end well for those persistent and pestering suitors.

But here's the magic for me of storymaking – a magic I've tried to pass on to children all my teaching life: this story was to have a new life, something that might make the hair stand up on the back of your neck.

Clare and I went to Ithaca three years ago, simply on holiday, not for research. I find that research is so often happenchance, not intentional. We were staying in a small house on a pebbly beach called Dexa, near Vathy, the main town on the island. And what did we discover? We found out we were staying on the very beach that Odysseus walked up when he came back from the Trojan Wars after ten years to reclaim his wife, Penelope, and his kingdom, disguised as a beggar.

We went to see his supposed palace. We walked amongst the olive trees, climbed the huge stones still there and took our photos, the bleating sheep all about us, their bells tinkling, the smell of thyme in the air. And we visited Homer's house too, where no doubt he had written his great stories, where he had walked and talked and lived out his life. All that was left of his house now were great tumbled stones, and amongst these legendary stones were growing ancient olive trees. I picked a legendary olive, almost the same olives

PERCHANCE TO DREAM

Homer must have eaten. I've planted one of them back at home in Devon – but that's by the by. One day, when I'm very old, I'll be able to eat one of Homer's olives and write my own *Odyssey*!

That same evening, there was a magical happening, a true happening. Promise. We were back on our beach. We were reading. Hardly anyone was about. I was reading *The Odyssey*, of course, in a wonderful new translation by Emily Wilson, when we noticed an old lady dressed in black walking slowly along the seashore. We'd seen her often with her family coming down on the beach in the cool at the end of the day. She was doing what she always did. She was keeping the beach clean of any plastic washed up in the shallows.

She stopped suddenly and waved us over. She was bending down, picking something up as we came closer. She was holding it out to show us in her cupped hands. It was a flying fish. It lay limp. Neither Clare nor I had ever seen one before. It was silver and glowing in the evening sun. Then she spoke, in halting English.

'It is dying,' she told us. 'They are washed up here on my beach quite often.' She held it a little closer to us. 'They talk, you know,' she went on. We must have looked doubtful.

'It is true,' she said. 'Listen.' And she stroked the head of the flying fish very gently with the back of her forefinger.

FUNNY THING, GETTING OLDER

The fish opened its mouth and uttered little plaintive sounds, again and again. The fish was speaking to us, trying to tell us something, something important. Maybe it was about dying, I thought. And then I thought something else, prompted I am sure, by having just visited the home of Homer, having lived with the story I had been reading, his story of all those gods, all those heroes.

I wondered and I thought: this beautiful silver flying fish must be, has to be, Proteus, the Greek god, who can turn himself into any creature he likes. And he is trying to tell me something. He wants me to tell a story about him and this island, its people and its tortured history, from ancient times to modern times.

That very same evening, after supper in a taverna, we were walking home round the bay in Vathy, talking about little else except Proteus, our talking fish, when we passed by a modern-looking house with a verandah. Sitting there was an old man, a drink in his hand. I greeted him in my best Greek. He replied in broad Australian 'Hello'. We stopped to talk. I asked him what an Australian was doing on Ithaca. He told me his life story.

Here it is. He grew up on Ithaca. In 1954, when he was a boy, there was a terrible earthquake on the island. Many died, much of the island was reduced to rubble. The boy, now alone in the world, became a refugee. He was sent to Australia where he had an uncle living in Melbourne, his only living relative. There he lived and became a Greek Australian. All his life he'd had this idea, a determination, to make his fortune and go back to Ithaca, rebuild his family home and then spend as much time as he could in his retirement on Ithaca.

In one day I had been gifted two wonderful stories – one rooted in an ancient legend, the other in a legend of our time. I fused the two and made it my own. I called it *When Fishes Flew*. I think it might be just about the only story ever told by a fish, a fish who is a god, with an Australian heroine who is not!

It is out of such myths and legends, ancient and modern, that we make our stories. I know that for sure. Every one of these tales has of course a specific origin – a place, a people, a language that created it. But every one is also universal, and once we have read it, belongs to us because we have lived it and imagined it.

We will, because of these stories, go on learning, wondering, dreaming and searching for wisdom and truth.

Recently, I wrote a story. It's a story of war and of a longing for peace. Relevant now, always relevant. And universal.

FUNNY THING, GETTING OLDER

Sadly. Sometimes it happens that the thread of a story has its origins in a land I've never been to, a people I do not know, and I find a need to weave their story into a story of home and us.

This story I called 'Our Tree of Hope', one story in a book of stories and poems I titled *But My Heart Was a Tree*. It's the best line in the book. I borrowed it, with permission. The line was written by Ted Hughes. He loved trees. So do I. We both lived in hope. I still do.

Our Tree of Hope
We used to play in the park, build our snowmen there, have picnics under our favourite tree, a weeping willow tree it was. Papa often called it 'our family tree'. I could reach up and stroke the green of her leaves in summer, the gold of her twigs in winter.

But then we had no park. We had craters instead. Then we had no tree. We had a wreck of a tree instead, a shattered splintered trunk, a broken crown of golden twigs. We used to have a town. We used to have a home. But then we had ruins and rubble instead. I used to have a father but he went to the war, and we didn't know where he was.

We lived in a basement. Every bomb that fell shook my bones, made Mama hold me ever tighter. There was no more food. There was no water to drink, but rainwater from the puddles outside. In the basement we sometimes sang songs so we didn't have to hear the planes coming over, the sound of gunfire in the distance, the sound of moaning and crying. We sang so we didn't cry ourselves.

We were in that basement for two weeks. It wasn't all a nightmare. We came out into the daylight sometimes when there was a pause in the bombing. There was sun and cold fresh air then, and often the brightness of new snow. We breathed it all in. There were dogs wandering around looking for food. Some of the houses were not even there. They'd been disappeared.

We walked back home every time we went out and searched the ruins for anything we could find. One day I found Papa's pen-knife in the rubble, and Mama found the headscarf Papa had given her the Christmas before the invasion happened, before the Russians came, before our whole world changed. The scarf was covered in dust, hardly recognisable. She was holding it to her face and crying into it. I put my arms around her, but I didn't cry. I was too sad these days to cry.

A shell fell on the outskirts of town. The ground shook, but I hardly bothered. I'd got used to the fear in the end, numbed by it perhaps. Mama had got through these dark

FUNNY THING, GETTING OLDER

times, I think, by worrying about me, and Papa; and I had got through by worrying about her, and Papa. Worry is useful. It distracts when you're hungry and thirsty and cold, and sad. Sad I never got used to. It saddened my heart every time we walked by our fallen tree. I never passed it by without reaching out and stroking her golden crown of twigs.

I was doing just that one early morning, wondering at the beauty of our family tree, even in death, how she glowed in the sunlight. That was the moment Mama told me.

'We are leaving, Katya. Today. Now. Don't be upset. Papa will know where to find us. If the worst came to the worst – and with the Russians shelling us like they are, it couldn't be much worse – we agreed that you and I would have to leave. The time has come.'

I wasn't too upset. Most of my school friends had left long ago. Anything was better than living in the basement waiting for the next bomb to fall. I just wanted to get away from the shelling, get away from the Russians.

'Where can we go?' I asked her. 'Where will we live?'

'England, you have your Aunt Aneta living there, and your Uncle Robert, they want us to come and live with them until we can find a place of our own.'

But I wasn't paying that much attention to her. All I was thinking about was that I wanted to take something from

PERCHANCE TO DREAM

Ukraine with me, something that was living, part of the land, part of my country.

I took out Papa's pen-knife, and told Mama what I wanted to do. 'You told me once that all you had to do to grow a willow tree like our family tree was to cut off a golden twig and plant it in the soil, make sure it was watered, and it would grow. Like magic, you said. That's what I want to do, Mama.'

She helped me choose the right golden twig. I held it while she cut it. I picked up a handful of Ukrainian earth, pressed it into a plastic cup we found lying nearby, and pushed the cutting deep in. Back in the basement, we wrapped it in a plastic bag, and put it carefully into a side pocket of my rucksack.

That cutting came in my rucksack with us all the way from home to Poland to Germany to France to England, and at last to Aunt Aneta's and Uncle Robert's house in Exeter, where I now live, for the moment, with Mama. We had quite a journey, I can tell you. We had to fill out more forms than – how do you say it? – than you've had hot dinners.

On the first evening we were there we planted the willow cutting from home in their lawn. I watered it every day, and it's already taken root. Mama was quite right. It is magic.

I go to school here now, speak English much better than Mama. I have English friends, lots of them. I sing in the

FUNNY THING, GETTING OLDER

school choir. And last week the choir sang the Ukrainian national anthem in Assembly, and that did make me cry.

Papa is still at the war. We phone each other often. They are doing well, he says. And they will fight on until the invader is driven out and sent home packing with all his tanks and guns. It may take a while, he said in his last call, and I must be patient. I'm not very good at being patient. But I'll try. I'm impatient to see him. I've just sent him a photo on my phone of our Ukrainian tree, and the English robin that perches on her and sings his heart out. I'm impatient for our tree to grow tall and strong, just like the family tree in our park at home in Ukraine.

Our tree is flourishing here, I am too. Mama misses Papa. We all do. We love it here, but we miss home. We will go back home one day soon, Mama says, to a free country, and Papa will be waiting for us.

Meanwhile we have our little reminder of Ukraine in the garden here, growing in Ukrainian earth and English earth. I like that. I love that.

She's our tree of hope.[7]

CORAM, HOGARTH, HANDEL AND MOZART

2017

About a dozen years ago, I was invited to a school near Berkhamsted to give a talk on creative writing to 'gifted and talented' secondary school pupils from all over Hertfordshire. It took place in the chapel at Ashlyns School. As I came down the long drive I was amazed. The school is a mansion, set in a great park of playing fields and trees. It is majestic and huge, brick-built with chimneys and cornices reminiscent of a stately home. I had never been to a state secondary school like it.

It was built in 1935 to accommodate the orphaned or abandoned children of the Foundling Hospital – the UK's first children's charity – when they moved out into the country from Coram's Fields in central London, until it was closed and the building became a school. The pupils showed me around their chapel, with its great organ up in the loft and a stage where, I supposed, the altar had once been. They took me down into the undercroft, which was flooded but still had old memorial stones brought years before from the

FUNNY THING, GETTING OLDER

Foundling Hospital chapel. I read the names of long-forgotten governors, including John Brownlow, a Foundling pupil who became its secretary and founder of the hospital's boys' band. Already in my mind's eye I was seeing this as a setting for a story.

I went back year after year to help with the creative writing away-day and every time explored the school more. I was becoming ever surer that I would write about this extraordinary place, once a home for abandoned children and now a regular secondary school with children of today living among the ghosts of their predecessors, singing in the same chapel, eating in the same dining room, the old dormitories now classrooms.

Eventually, I visited the Foundling Museum in Coram's Fields. The hospital, which continues today as the children's charity Coram, was founded in 1739 by philanthropist Thomas Coram. From 1741, when the first babies were admitted, to 1954, when the last pupil was placed in foster care, the hospital raised and educated 25,000 children.

I looked up in admiration at the founder's portrait, painted by William Hogarth in the eighteenth century. He was a remarkable and wonderful human being. History sometimes leaves great women and men behind and forgotten. 'The good is oft interred with their bones,' Shakespeare wrote. Thomas Coram was one of these. A shipbuilder and ship's captain, he spent much of his life in America where he worked tirelessly for the education of children, particularly Native Americans. He advocated schooling for all – especially girls – a remarkable thing in the 1700s. He was no sentimental philanthropist and wrote: 'I think and say it [education] is more material, for girls when they come to be mothers will have the forming of their children's lives, and if mothers be good or bad the children generally take after them, so that giving girls a virtuous education is a vast advantage to their posterity as well as to the public.'

Returning to London from America, Coram was horrified to see children starving and in dreadful squalor, small babies abandoned and dying in the streets. He refused to walk by and determined to do all he could to give these children life and hope. It took him 17 years of committed, single-minded fundraising amongst the great and good, including Hogarth and Handel, before Coram finally received a Royal Charter from King George II in 1739 to establish his Foundling Hospital.

The hospital was quickly overwhelmed with desperate mothers bringing their babies to the door. Each mother would leave a token, often a scrap of material cut from the baby's clothes, which could be identified if ever she came to reclaim the child, though very few ever did. She would keep one half and the other would remain at the hospital with the child's records.

Today, you can still see some of these at the Foundling Museum, each the start of their own story: a nut, a pot of rouge, a gambling chip, a button from the jacket of an officer in the Coldstream Guards, rings, bracelets, coins and handmade items such as embroidered hearts. On admission, each baby would be given a number and a new name (sometimes of one of the benefactors, so there were quite a few Hogarths), dressed in new clothes and baptised the following Sunday. They were sent off to the countryside to be wet-nursed and placed with foster families for their first years, growing up away from the stench and disease of the capital's streets.

Around the age of five, the children would return to the city to be given an education at the Foundling Hospital. From early on, rules were laid down about daily routines, bedtimes, meals and clothing for the Foundlings. At the hospital, they wore simple uniforms made of brown serge, which were still being worn on Sundays in the 1950s.

Great attention was given to ensuring the children received better than adequate – in some cases exceptional – care with regard to health, food and education. They themselves were responsible for much of the hospital's running, from dressing the younger children and cleaning, to drawing water and looking after the vegetable gardens. The farsighted Coram knew the children would one day need to earn their keep and so in 1751 he set up a network of apprenticeships for young foundlings in their teenage years, often amongst his friends and supporters. These usually lasted at least seven years; boys tending to follow careers in trade or the military and maritime services, whilst girls became domestic servants.

Despite his good work, Coram was not an easy man, by all accounts; few single-minded people are. But I was so inspired by him, by everything I saw in that museum – especially the tokens – that I followed up one or two leads, as story detectives like me are wont to do. And one of these led me to the eight-year-old Wolfgang Amadeus Mozart. William Hogarth used to look after many apprentices from the Foundling Hospital himself. I discovered he had a friend, Sir John Sullivan, who owned a large stately home in Kent called Bourne Park. Like so many benefactors, Sir John accepted youngsters from the Foundling Hospital as apprentices on his estate. It was also home to one of the earliest cricket pitches and locals played the game there, so it is not too much of a stretch to imagine apprentices might have played it there too. The more I delved the more excited I was

FUNNY THING, GETTING OLDER

becoming. Then came the great discovery, the moment I knew I just had to write my book.

It seems that in the spring of 1764, the Mozart family arrived in England after an exhausting tour of the continent with Wolfgang, the wonder child, being the main attraction. They came to recuperate for some weeks at Sir John's house. So Mozart came to Bourne Park, where there were apprentices from the Foundling Hospital. He would have met them, played with them, perhaps – cricket even! And Mozart was as mischievous as a boy, it seems, as he was as a man: cheeky, rather rude, funny and reckless, as well as brilliant.

The carpet of my story, that was to become *Lucky Button*, was already weaving itself; Coram, Hogarth, Handel and Mozart all being inspirational in the story-making. I just needed to sit at the loom and do it.

WAR HORSE

2016

I am not sure when the first seeds of *War Horse* were sown in my mind. That I was predisposed to be deeply concerned with war and the consequences of war there can be no doubt. But, like many of my generation, I was versed in my younger days more in the First World War than the Second. The first poetry that struck a chord with me was the poetry of the Great War: Owen, Sassoon, Thomas, Blunden. Wordsworth's 'Daffodils' and Keats's 'Ode to Autumn' left me cold at 15. I was taken to see Joan Littlewood's *Oh! What a Lovely War* and R. C. Sherriff's *Journey's End*, heard Britten's *War Requiem*. I read Remarque's *All Quiet on the Western Front*, Graves's *Goodbye to All That*. I saw *La Grande Illusion* and *Paths of Glory* at the cinema.

When I went to Sandhurst to become a soldier, perhaps, at least in part, I was seeking to prove myself. But army life did not agree with me. And it wasn't just the rigorous routine, or the bellowing of Sergeant-Major Bostock. I was coming to realise that this world was not for me, that this was not the road I wanted to follow. But I was unsure what to do. I didn't want to desert the great and good friends I had made in adversity. I was determined to stick it out.

However, one night out on exercise, in December 1962, something happened that made up my mind for me. It was bitterly cold, snow all around, biting wind. We were in slit trenches. Our 'enemies' across the wastes of no-man's-land in front of us were soldiers of the Argyll and Sutherland Highlanders, a Scottish regiment that seemed to us as hostile as any enemy could be. They were not pretending. They really did not care for officer cadets one bit, particularly ones like me, English and public school, and they made it quite clear what they might do to us if they could.

This of course was pretend war, but it reminded me – the snow, the cold, the trenches – of the First World War and Christmas Eve 1914, when soldiers on both sides climbed out of their trenches and met in the middle, and shook hands, and talked, and laughed together, and even played football. I think being there, and remembering that Christmas truce, confirmed in my mind that the way forward for me was not to spend my life preparing for war, but preparing and hoping for peace.

Eventually, I left the army, married young and went off to university, then from university into teaching, and while teaching found I loved telling the children stories, and that they loved it too. One day, I wrote one down and became a writer, a young writer struggling to find his voice. A writer's greatest source is memory, and my strongest memories were of my growing up. Both teachers, both lovers of the countryside, and disillusioned by the limitations of the classroom and school, Clare and I decided to fulfil our dream: to start a charity that would enable thousands of city children to spend a week of their young lives living and working on a farm. So, as you know, we bought a small estate in Devon near the village of Iddesleigh and began Farms for City Children.

Iddesleigh is a small village, about a hundred people, all of whom were very welcoming to the visiting children. We very soon got to know just about everyone in the parish, including three octogenarians, all old men who had been young once, at the time of the First World War. Two of them had gone to war, one just too young at the time to join up. One morning, in the Duke of York, the village pub, I fell into conversation with one of them. Wilf Ellis was now an antiques dealer. I had, a little while before, bought a picture from him, a nineteenth-century portrait in oil of a racehorse called Topthorn in his stable. But we didn't get talking about horses or pictures. This man, sitting across the log fire from me, beer in hand, had been to war, Sassoon's war, Owen's war. He had lived and fought in those trenches, faced the enemy and survived. I also knew he had never talked about it, and so he was hardly likely to talk about it now to a comparative stranger. Yet I heard myself saying: 'I heard you went to the First World War, Wilf. How old were you?' He stayed silent for a long while, looking into the fire. I was about to apologise and get up, when he said: 'Seventeen. I was seventeen.'

And then he went on. There followed an hour-long monologue of his time as a soldier at war, spoken in low tones, his language simple and direct, struggling with tears sometimes. He had been wounded, gassed, his life spared once by a German soldier. He spoke of his constant fear and sleeplessness, the cold, the wet, the joy of egg and chips and beer in the *estaminet*, and of a hot bath, the aching of his bones, the pain in his feet, the longing for home, for an end to it all.

Knowing already that my next story had to be about this war, Wilf's war, but having no sense of how to go about it, I went the next day to see Captain Budgett, the other First World War veteran and our neighbour down the lane. I sat in his sitting room. Here was a country gentleman, a former master of foxhounds, salmon fisherman, a man who could be gruff, I had been told. He was not gruff with me. Over tea, I asked him which regiment he had been in during the war. 'Devon Yeomanry,' he said. 'I was there with horses, y'know.'

He spoke in a measured way, seeing and feeling all he said. 'My horse, he was my best friend. I'd go to the horse lines at night and talk to him, my hand on his warm neck. And I'd whisper in his ear all those things you couldn't say to your pals, about home, and the terrible things you had seen, and the dread of tomorrow. He'd listen, y'know, really listen. True, I'm telling you. Best friends we were, him and me.' And this was not a sentimental man.

I went home and talked a great deal to Clare about how I might approach this story. She fetched down from the attic a series of gouache pictures. Her father had left them to her but they were not the kind of pictures she liked to look at. They were contemporary pictures of British cavalry in the war: in the horse lines feeding, in an extended line ready for the charge and one of cavalry charging up a hill into German positions, many of the horses already entangled in the wire. 'Maybe tell it from the horse's point of view,' Clare said.

I knew I needed to do a lot more research to find out all I could before I could ever find the voice for my story. I rang up the Imperial War Museum and asked a researcher there how many horses had gone to war.

'About a million, we think,' came the reply.

'And how many came home?'

'Sixty-five thousand.'

FUNNY THING, GETTING OLDER

The sums were easy enough to do. About the same number of horses as men had died in the war on our side. On all sides then, it followed that about 10 million men and 10 million horses had been killed – no one knows for sure. And they had died the same way: shellfire, machinegun and rifle fire, gas, drowned in mud, exhaustion, disease.

I went to see the last of the old men in the village who had lived at the time of the war. Albert Weeks had been a boy in the village when the war broke out, had worked with farm horses, remembered the army coming to the horse sale on the village green. Albert knew the land, every hedge and ditch, every field and stream in the parish, had worked on farms one way or another all his life.

The more I looked into it, the more certain I became that I did not want to write a story of this war simply from the perspective of one side or the other. That had been done often enough, and memorably. No, tell it differently; tell of the universal suffering of the war, as seen and experienced by some neutral observer and participant. And tell it in the first person, so that the reader lives it with you. A horse, it had to be a horse.

But still I hesitated. I did not want this story to be in any way mawkish or sentimental. Integrity and sentimentality were incompatible, I thought. How could I use the voice of a horse and not stray into sentimentality? I very nearly abandoned the whole project. Then something quite extraordinary happened that persuaded me I could do it, that sentiment and integrity are not incompatible, not in this case.

On the last night of the children's week on the farm, I would always walk up the lane to Nethercott House, where the children lived during their visit, to read them a story in front of the fire whilst they sipped their hot chocolate. This particular week, our guests had been from a school in Birmingham. It was a dark November night, raining. As I came into the stable yard at the back of the house, I saw a boy standing under the light by a stable door, in his slippers and dressing gown.

He was patting Hebe, our Haflinger mare, and talking to her. I was about to tell him to get inside when I realised who it was. The teachers had told me all about Billy. He was a very troubled child who, for one reason or another, either could not or would not speak. I had been warned not to ask him a direct question and expect an answer because he might take fright and run off home. And Devon is a long way from Birmingham, they pointed out. So all week, I had simply observed him. Billy kept himself to himself, never spoke a word, just got on with his farmwork. He did have a natural affinity with the animals and no fear of them, I had noticed.

FUNNY THING, GETTING OLDER

He had been first to put his hand under a sitting hen to pick a warm egg, confident driving the cows, at ease with Hebe. But never a word all week. And here he was now, talking nineteen to the dozen to Hebe, the words simply flowing, telling her all about his day on the farm. I went to find the teachers. They had to see this, hear this. We stood there in the dark witnessing this miracle, for that is what it seemed to be to the teachers. Then I noticed something else.

Hebe was listening, really listening. Her ears, her neck, her whole body language told me she knew it was important that she stood there and listened. Captain Budgett had not been exaggerating. Here was real friendship, trust, respect, love, and it was mutual. Here were two sentient beings communicating, each in his or her own way. There was genuine understanding between them. Completely convinced now I could tell my story in a horse's voice, with integrity and without sentimentality, I began writing the next day.

I struggled at times, but then I always do in my writing. I finished it in six months and the book came out, published by Kaye & Ward, in 1982, with a wonderful cover by the illustrator Victor Ambrus. Hopes were high, but soon to be dashed. It was reviewed hardly at all, and sometimes unfavourably. Then came the glad news that it had been shortlisted for the Whitbread Prize. My first time on a shortlist.

WAR HORSE

And *War Horse* was the favourite – the 'front runner' they called it. Dinner jacket on, Clare in her finery, up by train to London, limousine to the prize-giving, live on Channel 4. Roald Dahl, the chair of judges, stood to make the announcement. Not *War Horse*, not me. Some other book had won, some other beggar. Dahl was kind. 'Good book,' he told me afterwards, 'but children don't like history.'

There was no limousine waiting to take us back to Paddington. Night train home, sleepless. I was milking with the children the next morning. They had all heard about it and were very kind. 'We think you should have won, sir,' said one. 'Not fair,' said another. I just wished they would stop being so sympathetic.

Home for breakfast. Phone rings. Our good friend and neighbour Ted Hughes. He said nothing about the debacle of the night before, simply asked if I would like to go out for the day with him to look at bookshops in Bideford. We browsed together, still no mention of the prize I hadn't won. Then, over tea, he leant forward suddenly. 'Last night,' he said, 'that prize, none of it matters. Writing is not about winning or losing. You wrote a fine book, Michael. And I am here to tell you, you will write a finer one.' Wonderful words from a great writer and a wonderful friend – words that sustained me then and ever since.

FUNNY THING, GETTING OLDER

War Horse did not sell well. Fewer than 1,000 copies in hardback (which is why a copy of the first edition sells these days for such a fortune). Joey, the war horse himself, was pretty much forgotten, except by Clare, who, over the next 30 years and 120 more books, always maintained this was my best book – not necessarily what I wanted to hear whenever I gave her my latest masterpiece to read!

Then, out of the blue, in 2005, I heard that the National Theatre might be interested in making a play of *War Horse*. They had already produced, as part of Nicholas Hytner's enlightened drive to reach out to family audiences, Philip Pullman's *His Dark Materials* and then Jamila Gavin's *Coram Boy*, both of which had run highly successfully at the National for two seasons. *War Horse* might be next, I was told on the phone by Tom Morris, an associate director at the NT. I was thrilled, of course, flattered, but not a little sceptical. I simply could not see how *War Horse* could be staged. Then Tom told me. 'With puppets,' he said. My heart sank. Puppets, pantomime horses, playing out a First World War story? He sensed my disappointment, my disillusion. 'Come up to London, Michael. I'll show you the work of Handspring Puppets,' he said. 'You'll be amazed.' I went and I was. I watched, on a small screen in his office, a black-and-white film of a life-sized giraffe loping across a studio floor, manipulated by three puppeteers who almost at once became invisible. I found myself in tears as I watched. This was not simply a giraffe I was watching, but the spirit of giraffe and man together, in union.

I later learnt that it was Tom Morris's mother who had proposed *War Horse* to Tom. She knew he had been on the lookout for a year or more for a story that might enable him to bring the remarkable work of Handspring Puppets to the Olivier stage at the National, a story with an animal hero at its heart. His mother had happened to be listening to *Desert Island Discs* and heard some writer with an unpronounceable name going on about a book he had written called *War Horse*. She was interested, partly because Tom's grandfather had been to the war as a cavalryman. She went out at once, got a copy and read it. 'Just what you've been looking for, Tom,' she told him. 'You should read it.' Tom did what his mother told him and I am rather glad he did.

It took two years of workshopping and rehearsal. This was to be a groundbreaking production – not a play, not a musical, but a daring theatrical happening that defied definition. The directors, Tom Morris and Marianne Elliott, brought to the project a gathering of supreme talent – amongst them, Nick Stafford to write the script, Rae Smith to design, Adrian Sutton to compose, John Tams as song-maker, Basil Jones and Adrian Kohler of Handspring Puppet Company, and with them a company of extraordinary commitment and talent. But even then, after all that time and effort, they had underestimated the complexity of what they were trying to achieve, and things were not quite right by the first preview in 2007. A week's intense and anxious reworking and cutting followed, with Nicholas Hytner in attendance, and press night turned out, to everyone's great relief, to be a huge triumph, the reviews glowing. The NT had a hit on its hands. The Olivier was soon booked out for months ahead.

Two years later, having garnered numerous Olivier awards, and others, the show transferred to the New London in the West End, where it has played ever since. Seven million people have now seen the play worldwide. It was beamed on NT Live into packed cinemas all over the world, and it is currently still playing in London and in Beijing, the first ever collaboration between the National Theatre of Great Britain and the National Theatre of China. It has been the most successful production in the history of the National Theatre.

And Joey has become a star in his own right, putting in appearances at festivals, racecourses, old people's homes and national remembrance ceremonies all over the country, even in his home village of Iddesleigh. And he was famously there on the rooftop of the NT, rearing and whinnying, as the Queen sailed by on her barge during her rain-soaked trip down the Thames as part of the diamond jubilee celebrations. She clearly liked what she saw. She has a keen eye for a horse, and she and Joey are old friends. He even went to see her at Windsor once.

And so, from stage to screen. Kathy Kennedy, Steven Spielberg's producer on so many of his great films – *E.T.*, *Schindler's List* – happened to be in London and saw the play was on at the New London. Her daughter was keen on horses. They went to see it. Like so many, Kathy was overwhelmed by the power of the play, immediately contacted Spielberg and suggested he fly over. He came. He loved it too. He talked to the actors, went to visit the Imperial War Museum, met with Clare and me. A year later, he was making the film, and some of it in Devon, too. Clare and I made an appearance as extras; easy to miss it may have been, but at least we didn't end up on the cutting-room floor.

When the film came out, the book, which so few had been reading for all these 30 years, went straight to the top of the bestseller lists both in London and New York, and has now been translated into more than 40 languages. A source of great pleasure to me, of course, but of some irritation too. It was the same book, after all!

FUNNY THING, GETTING OLDER

In March, after seven wonderful years, Joey will finish his run in London. He will have a bit of a rest after all his exciting exertions, be put out to pasture back in Devon, where he was born and grew up. But it is not the end of the *War Horse* saga yet. From 2017 to 2019, Joey will be back out there again, trotting around the UK on his farewell tour. He will love that, so will the NT, so will we, so will the audiences. And after it is over, I console myself, the book will still be there. But, more importantly, we shall all have our memories of that night at the theatre when we first saw little Joey becoming big Joey before our eyes, when we first heard the cast singing 'Only Remembered', when we witnessed Joey entangled on the wire and the two soldiers, one a Fritz, one a Tommy, tossing a coin to see which of them should take Joey away and look after him, and then shaking hands afterwards.

Postscript

I just wish Wilf Ellis, Captain Budgett and Albert Weeks had been here to witness all of this, that they could see the show, which in the autumn of 2024 is about to begin yet another 18-month tour of the UK. Their story is still being told.

LISTEN TO THE CHILDREN

2019

The first book I ever produced, some 50 years ago, was a collection of poetry written by children. I called it *Children's Words*. There are poems in there by the young Daniel Day Lewis and Montague Don, amongst others, and another by one Samuel Taylor Coleridge.

I was a young teacher trying all I could to help children find their voices. It was at a time when teachers were not so confined to and driven by a narrow curriculum, the children not so taught to the exam, not so force-fed. So teachers like me could all have more time and space to explore ideas, discover worlds, write our poetry, tell our tales, sing our songs, paint our pictures, make and act our plays. It was a good time to teach. The work the children were producing was extraordinary; I was already beginning to realise, just how immense was the potential and talent of these young people. I should have known. I had children of my own.

What had not occurred to me so much then, but has become much more apparent to me now, and to all of us, I suspect – and has been one of the great and important benefits of social media – is the power of young people to change lives, change the world and how we see it. Patronise if you dare! The determination and courage of the young to take on the adult world – its hypocrisy, its greed, its idiocies, its hubris, its self-delusion, its ignorance, its absurd preconceptions and prejudices, 'to bravely go where no one has gone before' – has taken most of us by surprise.

Some of us might not have thought that young people had it in them. Some of us did not think they were old enough, that they would understand such things. And some did not think they had a right to stand up for their beliefs, to write what they feel, to do what they think is right, and say what should be put right. It wasn't long ago that there were some who thought of women that way. That's worth remembering.

Worth remembering too, is the contribution millions of children today are making the world over, towards the lives of others, towards this good earth, towards human rights, towards peace and reconciliation.

Let me mention just three of the millions who have made us sit up and think and change, who are telling us straight how it is, who are pricking our consciences and showing us a new way forward, a better way.

LISTEN TO THE CHILDREN

In Pakistan, some ten years ago now, Malala Yousafzai, a young schoolgirl of 11, was speaking out for the rights of all girls to be educated, and educated well. In full knowledge of how some in Pakistan might object to this – the Taliban in particular, and others – and understanding what risks she was taking, she went on speaking out. Her blogs for the BBC became well known. And the Taliban came for her, to silence her. They shot her in the school bus on her way home.

The assassination attempt backfired. After long months in hospital with all the world looking on through social media, all of us young or old wishing her well again, the doctors worked miracles and Malala recovered. And once recovered, she simply went on where she had left off, flying the flag for the rights of girls the world over to be educated.

And now, of course, the world was listening, applauding. She spoke at the United Nations. They have their Declaration of Human Rights. But standing there before them was a young girl from Pakistan who had nearly lost her life for those rights. She received the Nobel Peace Prize, the youngest ever to receive it. A child had changed the lives of others, changed the world for the better.

Then comes along another young girl, Greta Thunberg, 15, who decides enough is enough. She can see how climate change is threatening, how Sweden, her country, supposed, ecologically speaking, to be the most enlightened of countries, is not moving nearly fast enough in the reforms that need urgently to be made. In school, her teachers are telling her to switch off the lights and save the planet, and then they fly off all over the world for their holidays. Against all advice from parents and teachers, she goes on strike from her school, sitting in the street beside her banner. When asked why, she replied, in her own parlance: 'I am doing this because you adults are shitting on my future.'

This rang a bell for young people all over the world. Here was one of their own, brave enough to face up to the adult world that they knew was being hypocritical. This was their world that was being systematically polluted, exploited and destroyed. Young people are aware of the power of social media, know how to use it, and they used it. Millions of children went on strike from school, marched in the streets. The great and powerful, the politicians and the establishment, may have shaken their heads in disapproval, but they knew well enough that they had been rumbled, that Greta was right, as were her supporters, who will very soon be voters.

Greta has just sailed across the Atlantic to bring her message to the USA. She does not lack courage. Atlantic storms or President Donald Trump, she faces them down in

LISTEN TO THE CHILDREN

her own manner, quietly, firmly, politely. She is championing a great cause: to end climate change before it is too late, NOW, because it is an outrageous injustice to the planet and a cruel injustice to future generations. This is a cause the young all over the world have taken to their heart, and quite a few million old folk like me. We could not wish for a better champion.

And now to a hidden injustice I knew little or nothing of, until I met a young boy called Jonathan Bryan. He was ten when I met him. He has suffered severe cerebral palsy all his life. He has locked-in syndrome. He is entirely reliant on his family and his carers, and on 24-hour medical support, life support, effectively. He hears, he sees, he feels, he smiles. But he has no ability to speak at all, so could not communicate. Well, that's what people often think about such children, why people often give up on them.

His mother and his family thought otherwise. For too long, Jonathan simply existed. He would lie there in a room, the television on, with other children similarly afflicted. His mother knew there was a child in there longing to communicate, that Jonathan had a spirit, a mind, a personality, that he wanted to express himself. Between his mother and his carer and Jonathan, they found the key to unlock this locked-in boy.

FUNNY THING, GETTING OLDER

Jonathan could blink, he could move his eyes. He learned to spell out words, blinking at letters on the board his carer held out in front of him. It took years of practice to make the words make sentences, make conversation, make writing, make poetry, make a book – his first book, *Eye Can Write*. And can he write! And can he speak! I should say so.

I've known him for four years now. When I first met him, I did not know what to say. I knew he was a poet. All I could manage was a rather awkward: 'It's good to meet a young writer.' And he replied slowly, in his own blinking way: 'And it's good . . . to . . . meet . . . an . . . old . . . writer!'

I never patronised Jonathan again.

It was not good enough for this remarkable boy to learn to speak with the blink of an eye, not good enough to write a book. No, Jonathan Bryan began a campaign. He went to see ministers, talked to those who can make things change, went armed with a persuasive statement and an insistent demand which has important implications for the education of all children everywhere. His message is simply this. 'Never underestimate a child's potential. Give us the teaching, give us all we need to fulfil ourselves, to make the best of ourselves. Look at me. I had the help, support and encouragement I needed. And I can write. And with my writing I can change things, change lives. I can make a difference.'

LISTEN TO THE CHILDREN

Three children, all of whom found a voice of their own, a mission of their own, had the courage to endure and to speak out, and made the lives of others immeasurably better.

Listen to the children. It's their world as much as ours. More, really. They'll be here longer.

SEARCHING FOR WONDER

A FINE NIGHT, AND ALL'S WELL

2012

I wondered and I mused and I dreamed a lot when I was young. The place where this story happened was a place of dreams for me.

I was new, a new boy, a young boy in an old school – the oldest school in the country, they told me. Outside our dormitory window there was a Norman staircase and the medieval monastic buildings of the Green Court. Beyond that, there was the great cathedral itself and Bell Harry ringing out the hours, day and night.

We were expected to know the history of the school and the names of every building: house monitors could stop and test us any time. One of them – we already called him 'Flashman' (after the famous antihero) – would go on questioning us until we got something wrong. Then he would give us ten minutes to change into our PE kits, run around the Mint Yard a dozen times and afterwards report to him in his study, fully dressed again. The last task alone was almost impossible for us new boys as we were still all fingers and thumbs with our uniforms, trying to get to grips with wing collars and collar studs that seemed to have minds of their own. The uniform was part of the ritual of the place: boater, pinstriped trousers, wing collar, black jacket and waistcoat – with the middle button always done up if you were a new boy.

As new boys, we had to navigate our way through a sea of hazards. We learned quickly enough that the only way to keep out of trouble was to know our place, be on time and have that middle button done up. I longed simply to get through each day, to be in my bed and alone in the darkness. Only then could I put Flashman out of my mind and begin to dream that I was back home again.

But Bell Harry would remind me every hour, on the hour, that I was not. Lying awake, I'd listen for the night watchman to come on his rounds, pacing the precincts and the city wall. Sometimes his footsteps stopped right outside our dormitory window and I'd hear him calling out: 'Twelve o'clock. Fine night, and all's well.'

I took some comfort from that. Hoping it would be true for me the next day, praying that I would manage somehow to avoid Flashman and get through unnoticed and unpunished, I would fall asleep at last.

But my prayers weren't working. As the weeks passed, it

became obvious that Flashman had it in for me in particular. He used the strangeness of my name as his main weapon, teasing me about it every night. Then one night it got nasty. We were reading in the dormitory before lights out when I looked up and saw him there with his usual three cronies, standing at the end of my bed. I steeled myself.

'D'you know what someone told me, *Morpurgo?*' he began. 'Someone told me your name's Jewish. You're a Jew boy, aren't you?'

There was real menace in his eyes, naked dislike. I didn't argue. I didn't say anything.

'We don't like Jew boys, do we?' he went on. 'Gone all dumb, have we? Scared out of our little Jewish wits, are we?'

I am sure that worse would have happened had Mr Robbins, the housemaster, not come in at that moment to turn the lights out.

After that, fear of Flashman taught me wherever possible to go around in a protective band of others, a cocoon of friends. Perhaps we were all doing the same, finding strength and comfort in numbers. I wasn't the only one finding it difficult to settle into this strange place. I made these friends mostly on the rugby field or in the choir, singing Thomas Tallis or Orlando Gibbons in the cathedral or crashing through a tackle to score – life was getting better. I didn't excel at either singing or rugby, but did both just about well enough to be up there with those that did.

Schoolwork, though, was a real problem. I couldn't seem to make any headway and all too often I found myself in detention or playing catch-up, forever trying to explain why I had not yet done the work I should have done. For some reason, history seemed particularly difficult. It was towards the end of term that Mr Kennedy set us an essay on the murder of Thomas à Becket. I was struggling. We all knew the story, sort of: how the archbishop had been struck down in the cathedral in 1170 by four dastardly knights sent there by his erstwhile best friend, King Henry II. The trouble was that the essay had to be at least two sides long, and however large I wrote I hadn't been able to manage more than half a side. I did what I often did when confronted with a task I found too challenging: I procrastinated and worried about it.

My tutor, Mr Skipness, tried to help me. He suggested that for inspiration I should go and stand on the stone in the cathedral that marked the very spot where Becket had been murdered. He told me exactly where it was and how to get there. I couldn't help thinking at the time that it was a pretty silly idea, but I didn't say so of course, I just didn't do it.

It was nearly the end of term and the choir was practising hard for the carol service. Mr Hedred, our hyperactive genius of a choirmaster, gathered us for one last rehearsal in the undercroft of the cathedral, the crypt, our usual place for choir practice. It was a warm, dimly lit place of arches and flickering shadows – everywhere the scent of candles and ancient stone. I was sitting as always next to Peter, my best friend – fly half, and a brilliant one, on our rugby team – amongst the trebles. Peter had perfect pitch and a more musical voice than mine, which was fine for me because it meant that I could follow him.

We sang so well that evening that Mr Hedred ended choir practice early. He told us that we were the best choir he'd ever had, so we were all glowing as we stood up to go. That was when Peter told me that he had finished his Becket essay.

'Done yours?' he asked.

'Course,' I said.

None of the rest of this would have happened if I hadn't told that little lie.

That was when I panicked. In desperation, I decided I had no choice but to do just what Mr Skipness had suggested. As Peter and the others drifted away through the undercroft towards the door to the cloisters, I wandered off into the shadows and made my way up the steps and into the nave.

There was an echoing emptiness as I stood there, alone at the heart of the cathedral. I tried as hard as I could to calm my fears, thinking that if I turned back now it wouldn't be too late to catch up with the others – I could still hear the murmur of their voices. But then ahead of me, somewhere between the nave and the choir, I saw a flickering light that seemed to beckon me on. Without thinking, I walked towards it, down some steps and into a kind of side chapel.

Looking around, I could hardly believe it. It was almost exactly as Mr Skipness had described. There was the small square tile on the floor he had told me about. This must have been it, the very place where Thomas à Becket had been murdered.

I stood there and closed my eyes. In my mind, I pictured the knights bursting into the cathedral, swords drawn, and the archbishop telling them that this was a holy place and to put up their weapons. In horror, I watched as they hacked down one of his servants and then came on towards him. I saw him kneeling down, crossing himself and praying out loud as the first sword struck. The whole horrible deed was played out like a film in my head. I opened my eyes. I couldn't bear to watch any longer.

The man who stood in front of me was dressed like a bishop in a white cloak, his face shaded under a hood. He held a crozier in his hand.

A FINE NIGHT, AND ALL'S WELL

'You don't want to think about it,' he said, 'and neither do I. It was a painful business but over soon enough.'

The voice was far and yet near at the same time, the voice of a ghost. I ran. The only way out I could see was a small wooden door which I hoped might take me back to the cloisters. I lifted the latch. It wouldn't open. I hammered on the door.

'It's locked,' the voice said. 'Don't worry. I shan't harm you. Thomas à Becket never harmed anyone in his life. Why should he start now?'

I turned to face the ghost. He seemed to be floating over the floor towards me, caught up in his own source of light. He lifted his hood so that for the first time I could see his face. He was younger than I thought Thomas à Becket should be, with bright, smiling eyes. He held out his hand.

'They've all gone,' he said. 'Everything's locked up.' He took me by the elbow. 'But I have my own way out. Don't worry. Come along.'

As he led me through the vastness of the empty cathedral, he talked, answering all the questions I wanted to ask but didn't dare. When we reached the choir, he stopped and looked up at the high altar. He sighed.

'Henry was not a lucky name for me, not one I have any cause to be fond of. Michael, on the other hand, is a fine name.'

FUNNY THING, GETTING OLDER

'You know my name?' I breathed.

'I know everything about you, about everyone in this place. I've lived here, in one form or another, for nearly a thousand years. I've always made it my business to keep an eye on the place, to know who's who and what's what. I am able to go seen or unseen, as I wish, to look deep into hearts and minds – we can, you know. There's a lot I like about being a ghost. I'd rather be alive, of course I would; I died too young. But it doesn't matter now. What's a few years here or there? We're all of us a long time dead.

'Up there, just above the altar, that's where King Henry had me buried. You should have seen the tomb. Never saw so much gold in all my life – all to appease his conscience. He lay right there, flat on his face, and sobbed like a baby asking for forgiveness – as if anyone was fooled by his crocodile tears. And then another Henry, the eighth Henry, came along, dug up my bones and took away the gold. He was fond of gold that one, gold and wives. So you see, I have good cause not to like the name Henry very much.'

I was following him up the steep, winding stairway and finding it difficult to keep up. I thought that the steps would go on for ever, that he was taking me all the way to heaven. Then I felt the night air on my cheeks, and saw the stars and moon above me.

A FINE NIGHT, AND ALL'S WELL

'The top of Bell Harry,' he said. 'Look!'

Spread out beneath were the evening lights of the city and, right below us, the school: the Green Court, the Mint Yard and Galpins, my own house. I could see there was a light on in my dormitory, where Flashman, I was sure, would be waiting for me. Suddenly, I didn't want to go back.

The ghost seemed to anticipate my every thought.

'You mustn't worry about Flashman,' he said. 'One way or another, you'll find your own way to deal with him. And you'll finish that essay too. Which reminds me. Whatever you have heard, when those knights came for me – and you're right, they were dastardly – I didn't just kneel down meekly and let them get on with it. I fought like a tiger, wielding my crozier like a broadsword. I fought them to the end. The only way to live, and the only way to die.'

As he spoke, I felt his arm around my waist.

'You'll be fine, Michael,' he said. 'I've got you.'

And with that, we lifted gently off Bell Harry tower and floated down over the school, past the Norman staircase, to land right in the Mint Yard, just outside my house. I was so amazed and disorientated that I stumbled when I touched the ground. It took me a while to catch my breath.

'You all right?'

FUNNY THING, GETTING OLDER

I turned. It was the night watchman, standing there in the light of the lamp, smiling at me. But he was Thomas à Becket too. He had the face of the archbishop, the face of a saint.

'I'd best be off,' he said. 'Got my rounds to do. I like to keep an eye out.'

'What's it like being a saint?' I asked. It just slipped out.

'It doesn't cut any mustard, not where I come from. It's what you do you'll be remembered for, not the honours or the titles or the money. Just do the best you can. That's what I did. And that's all that I can tell you on the subject.'

He turned as if to go but then something else occurred to him. 'Except to say that you boys, you sang like angels tonight, like angels,' he said.

And with a wave of his hand, he walked away.

A window opened.

'Hey, Jew boy!' It was Flashman. 'What the devil do you think you're doing out there at this time of night? Go upstairs to your dormitory. Now!'

I got up early in the morning to write my essay on Becket and handed it in on time. When Mr Kennedy gave it back a couple of days later, he said, 'Entertaining, Morpurgo, but stick to the facts. Becket did not fight back. He submitted courageously to his fate. It is well known, well documented. You can't improve on truth, Morpurgo. Fiction is for fantasists.'

A FINE NIGHT, AND ALL'S WELL

As for Flashman, my moment to settle the score came a week or so later. We were out on the rugby pitch when I saw him come charging out of the scrum, ball in hand. I raced after him, chasing him across the pitch, and launched myself headlong at him. The impact knocked the air out of both of us. I was up first and glaring down at him as he lay at my feet. I didn't have to say a word. I knew from that moment on that neither Flashman nor his cronies would ever bother me again.

On the last night of term, after the carol service, I lay awake in my bed, listening out for the night watchman. As Bell Harry tolled the final stroke of midnight, I heard his familiar footsteps on the walk outside our window.

'Twelve o'clock. Fine night, and all's well,' he called out.

And all *was* well, too.

PLACES OF WONDER

2023

'When we came over the shoulder of the wild hill, above the sea, to Zennor, I felt we were coming into the Promised Land.' So D. H. Lawrence wrote when he first came with his wife, Frieda, to live at Tregerthen in Zennor in 1915. His two-year stay there wasn't entirely happy, but this was my impression too when we came to stay in exactly the same place for family holidays, 50 years ago now. Come over the hill today and nothing has changed.

Walking on Zennor hill above the village – they call it the 'church town' – and you find yourself on a high moor of gorse and heather, and in amongst great boulders sculptured by wind over thousands upon thousands of years. About you are ancient quoits, Bronze Age burial sites, and ruined, roofless cottages from the tin-mining era of Cornwall. Look out on a fine day over the patchwork of green fields spread out below you to the wide blue sea beyond, and to Zennor itself, a cluster of granite houses around the ancient church, and you might feel as I do every time I go there, that this is as close to paradise on earth as any place you have ever been.

PLACES OF WONDER

Listen and you will hear buzzards mewing high above you, or a cuckoo piping invisibly. Look up and you might spot a kestrel or a hobby or a peregrine falcon. It is a wild and wonderful world up there, where nature and weather rules. The wind can rage so that you can scarcely stand upright, and when the mists come down there is sudden silence and invisibility all around.

The place is full of legends. I made my own book of them and called it *The White Horse of Zennor*. Place is as important in my tales as people. It's hardly surprising that writers and artists love the place. Lawrence went to live there, so did Katherine Mansfield; the artist Patrick Heron lived on the moor and Barbara Hepworth knew it well.

Leave the moor and walk down the farm track past Tregerthen to the cliff path, turn right and in an hour or so you will be in St Ives, but my advice is to turn left, and within half an hour of walking you will be in Zennor. It is a pilgrimage for me every time I go to the church of St Senara, who was washed up on the coast nearby and founded the church in the sixth century. I find again the medieval carving on the end of a pew of the Mermaid of Zennor, and once more read her tale of how she came to the church and lured away a chorister whose voice she found irresistible.

My pilgrimage takes me from the church to the pub – the Tinners' Arms – for a pint of beer and a pint of prawns, to sit in the sun or in the mist, and feel the history of this ancient place all about me, soaking into me anew every time I go.

Often when I go to Zennor I am on my way to the Isles of Scilly – more for a holiday now than a pilgrimage – so I might spend a night near St Just, a mining village a mile or two down the road from Zennor. The people here are not just tourists like me; it's a real village with a school and even a great chemist. And I'll spend the last night on the mainland at the Gurnard's Head hotel, where there is always a great welcome, wonderful food and a snug room. Then, just down the road is Land's End airport, from where you can fly, lickety split, to Scilly, where if I'm lucky, I can stay at the Hell Bay hotel on Bryher and go walking round the island, see the seals bobbing in the sea off Rushy Bay, climb Samson Hill to discover again the cists of ancient chieftains.

Refreshed by the sea air, I can then go to my room at Hell Bay and write another book set on Scilly. I've written several now, from *Why the Whales Came* to *The Wreck of the Zanzibar*, to, most recently, *The Puffin Keeper*. Who knows where my next story will be set, Zennor, Scilly, Iddesleigh – where I do most of my dreaming, most of my writing – all places of wonder to me.

FUNNY THING, GETTING OLDER

2019

Funny thing, getting old, because I never thought it would happen to me. Well, it has, and quite suddenly too. Life these days is punctuated with little reminders. A certain reluctance, that I never had when I was young, when it comes to looking in the mirror. Full body or face. Neither merits a second glance.

Mirrors are in fact a perfect nuisance. In lifts with mirrors all round, sometimes you catch a glimpse of the back of a head that always lacks more hair than last time you looked, less than you had supposed or hoped. And a casual glance at a shop window as you pass by catches you walking more bent. Two choices. One: play the part. Beethoven, hands behind his back, bent into the wind, hair flying as he composes the Pastoral Symphony? Or you straighten up and walk younger, more youthfully, a sprightly step, just in case anyone else had noticed the elderly slouch. No one has of course, because no one is looking.

But I noticed. I do the Beethoven walk into the wind, humming the Pastoral. Good choice. In truth, of course, you

FUNNY THING, GETTING OLDER

hardly need mirrors to remind you that the years are marching on. There are plenty of other signs you can't avoid noticing. You have to think before you bend down to pick anything up or tie up a shoelace. There are baths too deep to get out of, so you have to turn turtle and push yourself up and out. But at least no one is looking. Then there are far too many kind people these days offering you a seat on the bus or the underground. Your little grandson outruns you easily on a country walk, and no longer just because you are pretending to let him win. You can pretend you are pretending, if you like, but he's not fooled, no one is fooled. I'm not fooled.

And these days, I'm finding there are far too many visits to doctors and nurses, wonderful though they are. Tests I was used to when I was young were vocabulary tests, comprehension tests, spelling tests. It's blood tests now. Then there's losing old friends, neighbours and family – I'm not sure you ever get used to being an orphan. That's maybe the worst of being old and getting older. There are more people you miss and with every one that goes, you are more alone. You find you are now amongst the last old trees in the park, wary of wild winds of fortune that might weaken you or uproot you. I'm sad sometimes that the world changes too fast around you and you feel you cannot belong, you cannot keep up. As a child I never liked feeling left behind. But you are in second childhood, Michael, I tell myself. Get used to it. Mustn't worry about sans eyes, sans teeth, sans everything. If it's another childhood you are living through, just be thankful for it. It means there's more ahead, more to look forward to, to live for.

So am I downhearted? No. What keeps me going are the young and the very old, the remarkably old. The young are beacons that burn bright with new hope, new energy, with the beauty of fervour, the joy of discovery. To be with them, to work with them, is to be inspired, feel the enchantment and excitement of youth again, to share it, to live in its glow. With them, around them, playing, talking, working, the years peel away. Age no longer wearies. When they've gone, I know they have tired me, but I sleep deep and wake contented, refreshed, younger in heart. Just as rejuvenating and energising to me are those who have lived long and never aged, some of the generation before me whose lives have been lived fully, who have stayed positive to the end, active, and who have contributed so much to all of us. They are my mentors. I will try to tread where they have trod, keep right on to the end of the road.

I think of Judith Kerr, author of *The Tiger Who Came to Tea* and *When Hitler Stole Pink Rabbit* and the Mog books, who passed away only recently, aged 96. She was at her desk

FUNNY THING, GETTING OLDER

writing and painting only a few weeks before she died. Well into her nineties she remained indefatigable, travelling widely, in this country and abroad, talking and drawing in schools, in libraries, at festivals, living life to the full. She walked four or five miles every day, ran up the stairs to her studio, loved to be with her friends, enjoyed good conversation and a good whisky last thing at night. She was a child refugee from Nazi Germany, had lived through family tragedy, through loss and grief, put up with living alone, worked through being alone. She had her memories, her cat, her family and friends. She loved making her books, meeting families and children who loved them. And what a legacy of joy she has left. If she was ever downhearted, and I'm sure she was, she just went on dreaming up her stories and characters, went on writing, painting, walking, running up her stairs, kept right on. I walk sometimes where she walked, along the Thames from Hammersmith Bridge to Putney. Just to think of Judith puts a spring in my step.

In the village where we live in Devon, we are a small community, with an average age of over 75. Every Tuesday lunchtime, the pub, the Duke of York, puts on a lunch for the older villagers. It costs £5 a head for a three-course meal. Twenty or thirty will turn up, a chance to meet, to talk of old times, to remember together. The village consists of a couple of dozen cottages, a village hall – once the old school, closed over 60 years ago now – the pub, the church, the chapel. It is a living community that has a strong tradition of looking after our old people. Families look after their own elderly as best they can, so elderly are looking after elderly more and more. It is a place where the old are valued, respected and cared for. And it is a place where I witness daily the courage and dignity of the old. They too are my mentors. I will try to emulate them all – Judith Kerr, and the old folk of my village.

And I'll keep right on.

I WONDER. AN EPITAPH

2022

I wonder what and who we need to look to in these dark times, in our perilous but miraculous democracy. Do we need anyone to be our president or monarch or prime minister or emperor? It seems, as most peoples do, we do. Historically, most societies have a need for leaders who can bring some kind of collective cohesion to our communal and personal lives, who can lift morale, stiffen the sinews, remind us of the best in us, comfort us through difficulty and disappointment, encourage hope and resilience, and rejoice with us when we have much to celebrate.

Now is such a time, now is always such a time. But our Queen of 70 years is no longer with us. It would be difficult to imagine a time of greater change in this world, in our country, than those 70 years of her reign. I don't have to imagine it. I have been there, millions of us have, as the country emerged from a war more destructive and terrible than any in human history – two world wars which were effectively one war with a 20-year break in between.

I WONDER. AN EPITAPH

The late Queen – and how hard it is now to say that – was born during that break, grew up under the shadow of the trauma and loss of the First World War, and was a teenager in 1939 when it happened all over again. She and her family did not escape to safety when the country was threatened with imminent invasion, when all seemed hopeless. They stayed and saw it through with the people, stayed calm and carried on. Not a nostalgic myth. Truth. They stood by that extraordinary generation, and yes, helped to keep up heart and hope when that was just about all there was.

When it ended, the young princess and her sister could go out in amongst the people, share the joy and the relief, and dance in the streets. They would have felt the same solidarity as the people, the same relief, the same hopes for the future, the same determination to make it a better world for everyone.

And so they did. As the clouds of grief and suffering lifted, a new optimism began at last to shine through. That young generation helped to create the foundation of the best of our world as we know it today – a health service for all, free at the point of delivery, schools for everyone and the slow beginnings of post-war prosperity. It was far from perfect; it is still far from perfect. But it was a start, the beginnings of hopes fulfilled. Mountains of all sorts were climbed, miles run faster than ever before, as all around bombsites were built over. The scars of war that could be healed were healed.

She was there with her father to open the Festival of Britain in 1951. There was rebuilding and renewal on a massive scale – schools, factories, theatres, new estates, town centres, shopping centres, hospitals, roads and airports. The pre-war world, the wartime world, became our world of today.

And young Princess Elizabeth saw all this, took it to heart and began to sense how her future might be, as her father rose to the unexpected and unwelcome challenge of having to be King. Her love and respect for him, and her faith, helped hone an unwavering sense of duty in one so young.

'The King is dead,' our fearsome French teacher told us at school one morning, and burst into tears. After the death of King George VI in 1952, I witnessed an entire people in mourning and realised for the first time how much he had been loved. The new young Queen committed herself to service to us, to do all she could. And that she has done, day after day, year after year, for 70 years, through good times and sad times in our lives, in her life, in the life of the country, as the world changed around us.

My classroom had a map of the world on the wall. A third of it was pink – that's us, our teacher told us. Only the blue

I WONDER. AN EPITAPH

of the sea covered more of that map. And I was told we ruled the seas too. It was already rapidly becoming fiction. The empire was dwindling country by country as I grew up, as the late Queen grew up. We ruled the seas now only when we sang 'Rule Britannia'.

The great wars had exhausted us, diminished our power irreparably. We were becoming what we had been before the days of empire – a small island off the European mainland with a remarkable language and culture, a unique and eccentric democratic tradition, and a royal family a thousand years old. Our rich history had left us, post-empire, as conflicted as we were proud. We were a country with an identity crisis, a society in constant flux, harking back endlessly and struggling, as we still are, to find a new place in the world, to discover who we as a people really are now. We seemed rootless.

The other constant was our late Queen. Throughout these turbulent decades, she struggled too, changed as we did, as we had to, but adhered always to the guiding principles of her faith, to her abiding sense of duty, whilst we often stuttered and stumbled into new era after new era, through triumph and disaster, through the seesaw years of prosperity and decline, into Europe and out of it, through massive social and geopolitical upheaval. She held fast to the idea that we were a people strong enough to find a way, to find ourselves, to come through. She gave us hope and comfort. She had seen worse times and she knew we had too, personally and as a nation, and had faith we would rise to the challenge. Her performance as Queen throughout the dramas of our times has been unerringly consistent and brilliant.

Her part in history was written for her partly by birth, mostly by circumstance – the circumstance being the abdication of her uncle. For 70 years and more, she played her part as Queen and directed herself in it. She had, every day, to be endlessly The Queen: stoic, politically knowledgeable and astute, personally gracious, wise, a good listener, thoughtful, adaptable, widely interested. To be a great actor on the public stage, but without ever seeming to be.

The hereditary principle sits uncomfortably with our parliamentary democracy. She knew that her role as Queen was only acceptable if the people admired and even loved her in the role. The crown and the jewels were costume, the palace was a stage set. She knew that; we knew that. She had no power, was not allowed to voice opinion. It was a charade, but one that worked wonderfully well because she was centre stage in our national drama, because enough of us believed in her.

We respected her and admired her because she worked hard, worked her socks off, and because she made us feel

I WONDER. AN EPITAPH

better about ourselves as a people. She seemed to know instinctively what to do about the dwindling empire. Reconciliation was at the heart of her faith, her thinking. She gave us roots again, roots still striving to take hold.

How do you bring together countries of the world who have been dominated by us, and more often than not exploited by us? By an acceptance of history, by a deep desire for reconciliation. She helped create out of centuries of empire a family of free democratic nations with a desire to strengthen and change historical links to one another. A Commonwealth. We know the late Queen thought this was the way forward for us and for them. She and her family worked tirelessly for it.

Many might believe this was merely a self-seeking ruse to cover up the cruelties and excesses of empire. I think the evidence contradicts this, that she would have nothing to do with such a ruse. I travelled to India in 1961 as a 16-year-old army cadet and was there when the late Queen and the Duke of Edinburgh came on a state visit, when Jawaharlal Nehru was prime minister – the man who, less than 15 years before, had led India's liberation from British rule. I was there on 26 February, Republic Day in India. Our Queen celebrated with them, tacitly acknowledging the contradictions of empire but also the warmth of a relationship that had survived. For her it was a journey of reconciliation, of respect and understanding. She was looking to the future. So were they. They wanted a future together. I watched her at work, knew she meant it.

Then Ireland. Is there a country anywhere, I wonder, where post-imperial peace has been harder to achieve, where our long and bitter history as a ruthless occupier is more deeply felt?

But it was the visit to Ireland of the Queen in May 2011, the first by a British monarch in a hundred years, that demonstrated to me vividly and unequivocally her commitment to peace and reconciliation. She looked squarely into the eyes of the Irish people and bowed her head. She went where it mattered most, to Croke Park where in 1920, 15 people had been massacred by the Royal Irish Constabulary. She went to the much-honoured cemetery in Dublin where many IRA fighters had been buried. For the Irish, these iconic places are sacred to the struggle for the liberation of their country. The Queen stood and bowed her head in acknowledgement. Irish people knew at that moment that there could be a future of goodwill and peace with Britain. And this from a Queen, we must remember, who had lost her uncle, Lord Mountbatten, assassinated by the IRA 32 years before in the Troubles. She shook hands with their erstwhile leaders. That we have peace

I WONDER. AN EPITAPH

now on the island of Ireland is due to her as much as anyone. She held out her hand and the Irish took it.

When we think of how many hands she shook in her lifetime! And for each one a greeting never forgotten. For each one a smile, a word or two for all of us in a crowd. Whatever our opinion of the monarchy, we know she did her best for all of us, to make this country, this world, better for our children. It's up to her children and grandchildren now to grow into the part and to play it from the heart, as she did.

They have had a wonderful example to follow, and so have we.

THE BOY WHO WOULD BE KING

2023

It was at about the same time as the wonderful National Theatre production of *War Horse* that Clare and I happened to find ourselves walking the countryside with the then Prince of Wales. We got talking about our mutual passion for nature and the countryside, and in our case about the children who come to stay for a working week of their young lives at Farms for City Children.

It wasn't difficult for the prince, growing up as he had, to imagine the impact such a week can have on young lives. The children leave with a new knowledge and understanding of where their food comes from, of the world of nature all around them. Look up and they might see a couple of mewing buzzards or swallows swooping overhead. Walk down along the river and they could see a heron rising or a flurry of ducks taking off. They take it all in, marvel at it and remember it. Moments like those become part of their lives and are sometimes genuinely life changing. They know they are part of this, that it is their world to enjoy and to care for. It is an important realisation.

THE BOY WHO WOULD BE KING

We talked probably too much about all this. But the Prince listened intently. He's a great listener. I went on about how the children dig up potatoes for the first time and, as they eat them, because they dug them up themselves, they are connected to them. It's same with the eggs they eat. Often, they'll write their name on the egg they've picked up from under the hen that morning so they can have it for breakfast. It is this connection, which has been broken over the generations, this personal nature of the relationship between us and what we eat, which is so important to recapture.

King Charles is of my generation but had more foresight about this lack of connection than me, and millions of others like me. He was telling us early on, in his twenties, that we were despoiling the planet, the rivers, the countryside, the air we breathe. He told us, and many mocked him mercilessly, ridiculing him as a 'tree-hugger'. Like David Attenborough and Greta Thunberg too, he was looking us in the eye and telling us, 'This is our world, and we are not here just to get fat and comfortable off it. We need to look after it. We must look after it because it looks after us.' That has been his passion throughout his life, and I'm full of admiration for his determination and commitment to the saving of our planet.

I've witnessed in others, as he has, the joy of discovering our closeness to all our fellow creatures, to the plant life around us on this earth. I see the deep pleasure in the face of my wife when she is looking out of the kitchen window at our bird table and watching the goldfinches and chaffinches flying in. I remember the wonder on the face of my son as he gazed down at a caterpillar on the palm of his hand. I know the pleasure I have in growing and picking vegetables. I feel part of everything around me, that I belong. Clare feels the same. We know how good it is for us to feel this strong sense of belonging, of togetherness.

King Charles has been speaking of all this for a long time. He was brave to do so. And he was right. We know that now he has been very much a prophet in his own land. At 21, just a year after his investiture as Prince of Wales, he used his first public speech to express concern about the pollution of our rivers and our seas, warning of the growing mountain of plastic pollution. And, sadly, little of this has been put right even now. In many respects, it's worse.

There's some who say that now he is king, he should keep out of the climate change issue, that it's too political. I'm sure he knows that and will be speaking out differently. But for all our sakes and the sake of the good earth, I hope he goes on making his point. I feel he must not be discouraged from doing this. The health of our environment, the danger of global warming, is certainly no longer a party-political

THE BOY WHO WOULD BE KING

issue, so it is perfectly legitimate for the King to speak of it. All political parties and a vast majority of the people in this country accept how important this is. The question of how it is to be resolved, the speed of the retreat from coal and oil, for instance, is political. The King knows the difference. It can only be helpful to the effort to sustain our planet Earth if the King continues to speak out and to set an example for us all.

We can all do something to help sustain our planet in our own small way, in our own lives. Do we really need to fly strawberries and blueberries across the world in February? No, we didn't before and it didn't kill us. We have bought into this idea over recent years that we can go to the supermarket and buy all these things all the time with little thought as to how it is affecting our planet. We should, we know, as much as possible, eat the produce that is grown close to where we live. In Devon where I live, we grow lots of leeks and potatoes. So we eat a lot of leek and potato soup, with croutons: delicious! It is no bad thing to have a new king to remind us from time to time that flying stuff around the world when we don't need to is not a good idea, even when we don't want to be reminded.

Queen Camilla has also proved to be a power for good in the land. She has been, in recent years, a fantastic

FUNNY THING, GETTING OLDER

ambassador for literature, a great ally in support of raising the profile of reading, particularly when it comes to children. She has worked tirelessly in this least prestigious, much neglected, but most important area of the arts. Our language is maybe our country's greatest legacy. We have given to the world wonderful literature and extraordinary theatre. Yet, in Shakespeare's country, one in four primary schools has no library, and there are far too many homes where there are no books. Whilst this dreadful and shameful neglect continues, we do at least now have someone in the royal household who speaks up powerfully for books and the joy of reading.

During the early days of the pandemic, I made a programme for BBC Radio 4's *A Point of View* about how our little village was a wonderful place to live because people genuinely looked after each other, and how important that was, especially at that time, because loneliness amongst old people in particular was becoming so hard to bear. I explained that in order to combat this sense of isolation, the old age pensioners would come to the pub for lunch once a fortnight at a price everyone could afford and have a get together. I said how beneficial this was for our old people. Someone at the palace must have heard the programme. They rang up to ask whether the then Prince of Wales and the then Duchess of Cornwall could join us to have lunch with all our pensioners.

So that is how the Prince of Wales came to make the first royal visit to Iddesleigh for a thousand years, and we all sat down with them to lunch in the garden of the pub and had a fine old time. It gave me a great insight into how genuine, kind and interested they are as people. It will never be forgotten in the village, that's for sure.

It was partly because of that extraordinary visit that, a year or so later, I began to write *The Boy Who Would Be King*. It's a fairytale of sorts about a little boy who knows he's going to be King when he grows up, and who has a passion for nature and wildlife. I hope he likes it. I hope they both like it.

DAWN CHORUS

2021

Written in lockdown.

I am too young to remember the war, just. But if there has been a Dunkirk moment in my life, it has been during the past year. Keeping calm and carrying on was no longer just some nostalgic historical slogan. It was what I was trying to do, we were all trying to do. What else could we do?

Instinctively, I knew I had to keep to a strict daily routine. Among other things, I became responsible for doing the breakfast in my home, which was why I was out in the vegetable garden one morning, in my wellies and pyjamas, picking kale and greeting the morning. I had been told by a dear friend that a kale smoothie at breakfast is very good for you. So is hope, I was about to discover. And so is song.

That morning, I heard a song, one that has helped to lift my spirits ever since: a blackbird perched on a branch high in an ash tree, singing his heart out. I stood there and listened, his song reminding me that it is a wonderful world, despite everything, and telling me that I was part of it, as he was, and not to be sad. Sing, he was telling me, and you won't be sad.

So I sang back to my blackbird, echoing his tune. Back and forth our song went, neither of us wanting to stop singing. He was there the next morning on his branch. We sang together morning after morning. I always knew he was waiting for me, and he knew I was longing to see him again, to sing with him again.

Today is International Dawn Chorus Day and like many of us I have never valued birdsong more than over the past year. In the early months of the pandemic, I was slow to realise the implications of what was happening. I tried to convince myself that the disease was far away in China, that it would never reach us and that, somehow, we were immune from such a catastrophe. Even when it overwhelmed towns in northern Italy, I still refused to believe it could ever affect us in this country, and even if it did, that we'd be safe in Devon anyway.

Then we heard that Denis Bater, who used to run the fish and chip shop for years in our local town of Hatherleigh, had died of it. At his funeral, the people came out onto the pavements all the way up the High Street to send him on his way. A dear cousin in Sheffield fell sick and was on a ventilator in hospital – she recovered but for some time we feared the worst. My best friend at university, godmother to one of our children, died in her nursing home and they said it was probably Covid.

The tentacles of this pandemic did of course reach down our little country lane where my wife and I live. Anxiety and fear crept remorselessly into all our lives, haunted our every day. Hope was all we had to cling to then, and I found it in that blackbird's song.

So it was that I sat down after breakfast one day and wrote my *Song of Gladness*, a story-song-poem that is passed on, one to the other, by every living thing on the planet, from blackbird's garden and my garden, all around the world, over oceans and desert sands, in rainforests and mountains, and back again to the blackbird in his ash tree. A journey in song over all the earth.

Making books, writing my stories, telling my tales has kept me hopeful all through the pandemic. I've had ups and downs, like most of us, but throughout, I've held fast to the memory of my blackbird's song, to my longing and determination to see family and friends again, and to my firm conviction that out of this we will come. When we do, we must grow closer to one another and to the world about us, never taking our planet, nor one another, for granted again.

DAWN CHORUS

When I wrote this story, it was during the early months of the pandemic. I sensed that if I let go of hope, I could so easily fall into a dark pool of sadness and fear and grieving that would drag me down into depression. Every morning, I would notice the world about me more; my blackbird was singing to me, the swallows were there and farming life was going on in the countryside all around us. Hope sprung, my spirits rose.

But of course it was not just a blackbird and a song that brought hope. It was the community too. We were finding a new kindness all around us, we were cocooned in it. Neighbours we hardly knew were taking us under their wings. They called in, they shopped for us, fetched medicine for us, became friends. Everyone who came by – the postie, the refuse collectors, the delivery men – had time to stop and talk, distantly, masked. And how we loved that. How healing and hopeful that was.

We lived in real hope now that we would see our children and grandchildren again – soon even, maybe. That before long we would see the city children out on the farm again feeding the sheep and hear their laughter in the wind.

How important a lesson that is to learn for when this is over and we can reclaim our lives again. We have seen the kindness in the eyes of our neighbours, witnessed the

FUNNY THING, GETTING OLDER

dedication of those who care for us, in hospitals and care homes, in our schools and homes. We have come closer to one another because we have rediscovered that we do belong to one another, that there is great kindness in this world, often right next door.

This morning, just about a year on, I was again out in my wellies in the garden, picking kale, when I heard my blackbird singing again high in his ash tree. He was reminding me that his song is my song, my song is his song, that his world is our world.

TAKING TIME

2023

It's mid-December as I write. When I went out into the garden to feed the birds this morning, I saw the goldfinches and woodpeckers were waiting for me in the trees. They are often there on cold and frosty mornings, watching me as I am watching them.

The feeding done, I am reluctant to go inside. The world about me is gold with the dawn, the valley white with frost and, in the distance, Dartmoor clear against a blue sky. There is stillness. And I'm thinking, cold and frosty morning, sheep safely grazing. Christmas. Christmas only days away now, family coming, children, grandchildren. As it should be. What is there left to get ready? Out on the farm, I can hear the geese being fed, and the pigs.

I remember then the goose Clare and I had picked out, and feel bad about it again, briefly. I walk past the Christmas tree that we recycle each year. I reach out and brush the frost off the top of it. I'll soon have to bring it in again, about the fifth Christmas it's been with us. 'Morning, tree,' I say, 'not long now.'

FUNNY THING, GETTING OLDER

Porridge seems seasonally appropriate and I'm good at making it. A quiet breakfast together, another list to be made, hot tea and toast, and I'm dressed and off on my walk, the walk that I know helped get me through to 80, that I hope will get me to 90. There are things still to be done, but they can wait for a little while, even at Christmas.

The frost is crisp and even, as I open the gate into the sheep field. They come running up for food. I tell them I haven't got any, that Simon will soon be there. And then I'm on my way across the field, the sheep following for a while until they give up. This is my daily walk, down through the fields to the woods ahead. I love the woods. I'm walking across the field now towards Bluebell Wood. In Ted Hughes' words, 'My walk is the walk of a human child, but my heart is a tree.' The cows here are already busy feeding on the hay that Simon has just left for them, their communal breath lingering above them as they eat.

My boots are dusted white with the frost, my hands and cheeks chilled, my nose too. The gate into the wood I have opened and shut a thousand times, but today it thwarts my numbed and clumsy fingers. Once in the wood, I look out for the deer, as I always do. They come often to drink at the stream and I love to catch a glimpse of them, of a white bottom or two, before they spring away. None today. Pity. On I go.

The carpet of dry leaves, acorns and beech mast crunches under my feet as I pass by the badger sett, look for traces of recent comings and goings. There's fresh earth dug out. There are down there, warm and safe, listening for me, no doubt.

I come warily to the clearing in the wood, where I tripped and fell heavily a while ago and hurt my shoulder, the same one I injured playing rugby when I was 16. Then it had been a criminally late tackle – not cricket at all. Last year, it was a root hidden under the leaves that had ambushed me. I see and remember the offending root and take good care.

Only a few weeks ago, it seems, there were mushrooms growing here, and in large numbers, but no longer. Too cold for them. The bluebells are lying dormant under my boots, taking their time, waiting for spring. They have a long wait ahead.

I'm out in the brightness of the hillside soon enough. I'm walking down the hill that I used to run down, that my children rolled down and now their children do the same, and their children too. In a few days now, they'll be here again and the fields will be ringing with their laughter. I won't race them anymore. I took a tumble last time. I'll stand and watch, and that'll be fine. I do that a lot these days, standing and staring. Time well spent.

And there below me is the shining river, the Torridge, and the magnificent stand of oak trees, filling the valley on the other side. 'Earth has not anything to show more fair,' William Wordsworth wrote of Westminster Bridge. Great line, but wrong place, Mr Wordsworth. I don't think Wordsworth ever came here to the Torridge, but other poets and writers did. Ted Hughes did, and Seamus Heaney, and Tarka the Otter's Henry Williamson too, amongst others.

It's on these walks that I invent stories, that I ponder and dream, and maybe tell them to myself out loud. I sing out loud sometimes too. No one can hear me down here, only the ducks and the herons, and they don't mind. The older I get, the more I like to sing. I was a choirboy once. I loved carols, still do.

This riverbank is full of memories, all of those who walked it before me, and with me, family, friends and the city children who came with us on their Sunday walk, the thousands of them who have come over the years for their week in the countryside, on the farm, a week of world-away that they never forget in a place where they can stand and wonder and dream.

TAKING TIME

For 50 years and more I've been doing this same river walk. It's the familiarity I love, the rhythm of the seasons, how it's never the same as the day before, how I always discover something I haven't seen or thought before, how my imagination takes wing.

Thomas Hardy called it 'the old association'. He had a way with words.

It's the life of the river that stays with me: the droughts that reduce it to a muddy trickle, the floods that roar and rage, and spread out to cover the water meadows. I love the calm on summer days with the dragonflies hovering over the water, the fish rising, salmon or trout or sea trout; the swallows and martins and swifts all there, sometimes all together, the heron still in the shallows, the bright kingfisher flashing by, gone before he was ever there, the buzzards circling the sun and moving over the hillside. All these I love.

And on days like today, there are always duck taking off in a sudden frantic flurry of splashing and quacking, circling round above me, annoyed that I have interrupted their peace. I walk on and they always come back to land close to where they took off. Will they never learn? I don't carry a gun. I never have. But how I love to look up and see them fly!

But in all this time, I had never once seen an otter. I've seen paw prints. I've seen spraints, otter poos – the children love saying that and searching the riverbank for them! I must, consciously or subconsciously, have been looking out for a glimpse of an otter on every walk I've made along the river. Not a one in 50 years.

I'm coming to the place now.

Only two days ago, I was walking happily along here, minding my own business, quite close to the bank where the old alder tree leans out over a still, dark pool. I've seen fish jumping there often before. I noticed the end of a salmon's tail disappearing into the water. Salmon or sea trout, I wondered which. So I stood there and waited for the fish to rise again. How glad I am that I stood and watched. How glad.

A fish didn't rise but an otter did. Tarka did. He looked up, saw me and went on chewing his catch between his paws. He dived again, slid down into the river, hardly making a ripple. I didn't move. I didn't breathe. A few moments later, up he came again. Again, and again, and again, sometimes with a fish or an eel, or maybe a mussel which he crunched hungrily. And each time as he ate his catch, he was watching me. His eyes met mine. Mine met his.

Over 80 times, I promise you, my Tarka dived and came up again. I must've been there for over 40 minutes, watching, before this momentous moment in my life ended and I had to accept my otter had hunted enough, was gone, and was not coming back. I felt suddenly very alone. But of course, Tarka was not gone. He was there. I was there. We had met. It was enough. That moment was not 40 minutes long, it was for the rest of my life. I knew that for a while he trusted me, had stayed to spend time with me.

It's the best Christmas present I ever had. I've thought about little else since. I shall take the family down there and show them the place. And you never know, I could get lucky again.

My way back home from the dark pool in the river where I saw Tarka that day is up the steep rutty lane with high hedges on either side, hedges first built by the Saxons, who farmed here a thousand and more years ago. Then on past the ancient granite cross, where the monks stopped to pray.

I hear the village church bells ringing in the distance, practising for the carol service probably. I used to ring the tenor bell when I was young. To play a small part in the making of such a joyous sound brings back wonderful memories. Christmas is so much about the gathering of memories. And music making, church bells or singing in the choir as a boy, has always been the heart of Christmas for me.

I'm hoping the carol singers will come on Christmas Eve. There may not be as many singers as there used to be, but they always sing the same carols we all know in the same spirit. It's where carols are best sung, I think, standing out there in the open air with friends and neighbours, all of us joining in. My favourite is not so well known, a gentle lullaby, 'Dunstan Lullaby', a reminder that Christmas for many is time of togetherness and family and fun, but it's also a time to reflect and wonder, a time to celebrate the birth and life of a refugee baby cradled in a manger of straw in a stable all those centuries ago, who brought us hope, hope for peace and goodwill.

A LETTER FROM GRANDPA CHRISTMAS

2018

I felt properly qualified to write this. I'm a grandpa to eight grandchildren and a great-grandpa to three great-grandchildren.

I'm quite a traditionalist at Christmas. Like so many, I like there to be at least some echoes of family Christmases past: the tree, the presents, the decorations – many of them handed down by my grandparents – church on Christmas morning, the carols, goose, sprouts – yes, sprouts! – and roast potatoes, and for afters, Christmas pudding aflame with brandy.

And stories are an integral part of it all. Yes, I'd say more books are given as presents than anything else. But I don't mean that. I mean stories, beloved stories are read again, watched on television again – *The Snowman*, *A Christmas Carol*, *Paddington*, *The Night Before Christmas*. And I've written one or two of my own.

Increasingly, deep in my grandpa years, I find myself contemplating my past Christmases as a child. I often wonder as I watch the children playing, reading, laughing and squabbling maybe too, lost in the magic and excitement of it all.

But I have been finding that in the autumn of my life, I'm more contemplative at Christmastide, and writing that way too. Joys are heightened by having the children about us, but so are sadnesses. So many of those we've known and loved were with us at Christmastime, all the way through our lives. We miss them so much more sharply at Christmas.

We know more and more as grandparents how lucky we are to have enjoyed so many Christmases watching the children growing up. We want the best for them, of course, long life and happiness. We want them to live in a world not torn by war, to live in harmony with one another, and just as importantly with the world about us, the wonderful world we have so damaged, that we have so long taken for granted.

So I wrote a story about a grandpa like me – actually, who is me – deciding to write a letter to his granddaughter, Mia. It's a wish list for a better world, a world of peace and goodwill. I wrote it on Christmas Day a while ago now. It's a wish list for Mia in my story, but in truth for all our grandchildren and great-grandchildren, for yours too, and for children the world over.

—

A LETTER FROM GRANDPA CHRISTMAS

A letter from your grandpa, who you call Grandpa Christmas because you see me every Christmas.

Dearest Mia,

Have you ever seen a picture of us, of this Earth of ours, from space, Mia?

We are a bright blue bead, spinning through infinity. A beacon of life. But one day, if we do not care for her, this good Earth of ours will be as arid and lifeless as the moon.

The life of this world is as fragile as you are, as I am, as trees are, as butterflies and bees and birds are, as worms and frogs are, as plants are.

If I have learnt one thing for sure in my long life – 80 this year, Mia, and that's old – it is this: the Earth is a living, breathing being and we must hurt her no more. We are using her up, fouling the air and the sea, making a dustbin of the land, a sewer of the oceans, a graveyard of her creatures.

We have to learn to love our dear Earth again, Mia, love her, as much as I love you and you love me. For, you and I, we are part of this living planet, part of Earth's great family. And we are her guardians too.

So I wish for you, little Mia, and for all children everywhere, a new world, without war, or waste, where children

FUNNY THING, GETTING OLDER

like you will be able to breathe in good, clean air and drink from clear, bright water; a new time when we grow and eat only what we need, no more, and learn to share all we have, so that no one anywhere goes hungry ever again.

I wish no tree ever to be cut down without planting three more in its place. I wish for you a world where in flying our planes, driving our cars, heating our homes; where in our endless striving to be ever more prosperous, ever more comfortable, we do not overheat the planet, do not melt the ice caps, raise the oceans, and so bring famine and flood and fire down upon ourselves.

I wish for you a world where the whale and dolphin and turtle, and the jellyfish, can live the life of the deep undisturbed, in seas unpolluted – those same seas, little Mia, where we have paddled and played so often on our summer holidays, do you remember?

I wish for you a world where the elephant and lion and the tiger, and the orangutan, can live wild and free, never locked up and imprisoned simply for our entertainment, but left to themselves in their forests, left to roam their plains and their deserts, left to live their lives in peace.

These we have loved together: the sea, the trees, the birds in the garden, the wriggly worm, the jumping frog, the good soil where we dig sometimes – where you help me grow my potatoes and my cabbages.

A LETTER FROM GRANDPA CHRISTMAS

So, look after all we have loved together. Live always in rhythm, in harmony with this Earth. Then all my wishes will come true for you, and all shall be well.

But all shall be well only if we make it well, little Mia. There is a lot of healing to do, a lot of loving.

Your Grandpa Christmas

POEMS FOR VIVALDI'S 'FOUR SEASONS'

2024

My way of life, my home in Devon, my walks on the wild side have kept me in close touch with the seasons, and so with Vivaldi's 'Four Seasons'. Only very recently, I found out that Vivaldi had written introductory poems for each of his four seasons, by way of explaining what exactly it was that had inspired the composing of the music, what he had in mind as he wrote it.

I mentioned at the beginning of this book how inspiring I have found it in my later years to be asked to write or perform outside my safety zone, beyond my well-trodden path of fiction, of writing for children. For some years, I have been involved in concert performances of The Mozart Question, *a story I wrote about the Jewish musicians who were forced by the Nazis to play in the orchestras in concentration camps. I read the story and the music is played by the violinist Daniel Pioro and the Storyteller's Quartet.*

Daniel told me one day about Vivaldi's poems and sent them to me to read. He wanted to create a new recording of 'The Four Seasons' and would I translate or retell Vivaldi's

POEMS FOR VIVALDI'S 'FOUR SEASONS'

poems so that they could be read and performed with the music? So I did.

Here are the poems, which I suggest you read as you listen to 'The Four Seasons'. They need the music. The recording has now been made, wonderfully played by Daniel and Manchester Camerata orchestra.

I hope you enjoy both.

Spring
Spring is sprung. Winter is done.
Sing out, you chirruping birds,
So we know it's true.
Sway and wave, you budding trees
Show us your glorious green, your early leaves,
Then we will have to believe, that
Spring is sprung and winter is done.

Silver stream in the depths of the wood,
Shine on, run soft.
Hear the distant thunder,
The crackle and roar.
Feel the cloud shadow, feel the rain.
And now the light of sun again.
Shine on, sweet stream, run soft.

FUNNY THING, GETTING OLDER

I listen to you diva blackbird, I see you flitting wren,
I hear you in the woods, drumming woodpecker,
I see you up high, mewing buzzard.
I see you, you hear me.
You sing to me, I sing to you.
We sing in perfect harmony,
For winter is done, and spring is come.

Summer
Welcome happy days of sun and summer.
Welcome back, you skimming swallows,
You screeching swifts,
You buntings and godwits,
How we have longed to see you again,
You found your way back.
You bring our summer with you,
Make your summer homes with us,
Be again our family and friends, lift our spirits,

Warm our hearts.

Here we are to greet you again.
Woken now from winter sleep.
Honeysuckle and campion,

POEMS FOR VIVALDI'S 'FOUR SEASONS'

Dog-rose and foxglove,
buttercup, and daisy,
Bright-eyed daisy by day, closed tight at night,
And every morning, every dawning,
Each one gladly opened up again,
By summer sun, by you.

As we are too.

Cuckoo calls, unseen, from far-off wood,
Summer's echoing herald.
Lark rises high in the blue, and is lost.
But her song still sings.
Hay dances in the warmth of the breeze,
Sways and waves with the whispering trees.
The world has come alive again.
And it is wondrous to us.
On days like this, sweet summer,

You make it so.

We may swelter often in the heat of the day.
As we shear our sheep and make our hay.
Summer storms may flash and rumble,

FUNNY THING, GETTING OLDER

And blow in wild on gusty winds
With squally hail and lashing rain.
They can roar and rage all they like.
We do not care. It cleans the air.
We are watered, filled with newness,
Like the fields, like the flowers, like the trees,

Like the whole wide world.

Autumn

Harvest home, all gathered in, all stacked and stored.
Hayricks high as the sky, larders loaded with all we need.
More mud than mist these days, more rain than shine.
Leaves to scuffle, berries and nuts to squirrel away.
Every day shorter than the last.
Every evening longer in front of the fire.
The wind sighs and soughs in the chimney,
The house hunkers down, heaves and creaks,
In the monster-gale that shakes windows and doors,
That whines and shrieks outside.

He can do his very worst.

Inside we sing, we laugh, we dance,
Remember work well done, and done together,

POEMS FOR VIVALDI'S 'FOUR SEASONS'

Have a glass of this, a mug of that,
Forget the dark out there, the grey days to come,
Tonight is for joy, we care for nothing else.
Stories and mugs go around, with more songs
The monster-gale is gone, we have laughed it away.
Danced it away, sung and drunk it away.
Ready for sleep now, and the house sleeps with us.
To bed, to fuddled dreams and blessed sleep.

Owl may answer owl. But we dream on.

The house slumbers and snores in harvest harmony,
Until dawn breaks, and wakes hounds and horses alike.
They know it's the day, let us know it's time
To mount up and be away to the chase.
They drag us out of our beds, startle forest and field,
Tell it out loud to fox and hare, to deer and boar.
They hear well enough the echoing horn,
And tremble at what they fear must come.
They know the thunder of hooves, the baying of hounds.
The chase is on, over ditch and stream and hedge, we go.

Halloo, hallo, halloo, hallo!

FUNNY THING, GETTING OLDER

Fox has long gone to ground.
Boar hides deep in his lair.
Hare skitters away, springing and jinking to safety.
Only stag, white stag, monarch stag,
King of the forest, turns and stands his ground,
Tosses away hound after hound,
Then wearied at last, runs from his mountain down to the rushing stream,
Too fast, too deep for the hounds, who can only bay from the bank.
Midstream he falls, heart-bursting,
His crown of antlers held high to the last above the water.

His end shall be told around our fires for years to come.

Winter
By night cold winter moon hangs up there,
By day pale sun brings us no warmth.
We are as frozen as the world about us.
Feet, fingers, ears, nose, ache with it,
Frost and snow, ice and sleet, no hiding place out there.
But we have hearth and home to huddle in,
To thaw ourselves out, feel toes again.

POEMS FOR VIVALDI'S 'FOUR SEASONS'

We have piping porridge, steaming soup,
A log fire ablaze, a warm bed, blankets.
At night each warms the other,
And the dog does too. We share our warmth.

We dream of spring, and wake to winter.

Winter white all about us. Puddles and pails frozen hard.
A forbidden lake iced over, beckons us.
We slip and slide, gambol and tumble.
Frisky with laughter and courage we test the ice.
The lake invites us, tempts us on, to brave the web of
   cracks.
One more tentative step may be one step too far.
Deep down there, a dark and icy grave.
We brave it only so far.
Back to snowman. Better to build a friend,
Make war with snowballs,
Than make a watery end.

What it is to be young again!

All of us now bright with laughter, faces glowing,
Not just with cold, with the joy of it too,

FUNNY THING, GETTING OLDER

Grateful now for this gift of snow.
And Christmas Day so nearly here.
When the year turns round once more.
Ahead of us the first snowdrop,
The lengthening of days and welcome sun,
New warmth, new life,
Then the swallows and swifts,
Coming home to us at last.

All will be well.

SOURCES

Great Expectations	*i-news.co.uk*, 24 December 2023
Owl or Pussycat?	*Daily Express*, 18 December 2020
The Happiest Days of Your Life . . .	*A Point of View*, BBC Radio 4, 6 October 2019
Let Me Take You There	*The Essay: Let Me Take You There* BBC Radio 3, 20 May 2020
Passing It On	Foreword to The Times Education Commission's final report , June 2022
All Around the Year	Introduction to *All Around the Year*, Little Toller Books, 2023
The Voices of Children	Published in *The Invention of Childhood*, Hugh Cunningham, BBC Books, 2006
Little Amal	*A Point of View*, BBC Radio 4, 17 September 2021
Set Our Children Free	The Richard Dimbleby Lecture, BBC Radio 4, 4 March 2011
Lucy Lost	*The Times*, 13 September 2014
The Tilth of Truth	*The Times*, 3 October 2015
Poppies	*Radio Times*, 9 November 2018
Imagine	*A Point of View*, BBC Radio 4, 27 July 2018
The Road to Peace	*A Point of View*, BBC Radio 4, 12 August 2018
The Phoenix of Peace	*The Times*, 20 October 2019
All the World's a Stage	*A Point of View*, BBC Radio 4, 21 March 2021

FUNNY THING, GETTING OLDER

The Violin of Hope	Address to the Anne Frank Foundation, 18 January 2024
Finding Alfie	*Telegraph*, 8 May 2024
A Strange Meeting in an Oxford Restaurant	*A Point of View*, BBC Radio 4, 26 July 2024
Will There Be Singing?	Talk for Making the Implicit Explicit Conference, Monkton Combe School, 16 June 2023 (with extract from *I Believe in Unicorns*, Michael Morpurgo, Walker Books, 2015)
Perchance to Dream	*The Gifts of Reading for the Next Generation*, Scribe, 2025 (with extract from *My Heart Was a Tree*, Michael Morpurgo, Two Hoots, 2023)
Coram, Handel, Hogarth and Mozart	*Daily Express,* 26 November 2017
War Horse	*The Times,* 21 February 2016
Listen to the Children	*Spectator*, 21 September 2019
A Fine Night, and All's Well	From *War Child to War Horse,* Maggie Fergusson, Fourth Estate, 2012
Places of Wonder	*Waitrose Magazine,* Spring 2023
Funny Thing, Getting Older	*A Point of View*, BBC Radio 4, 29 September 2019
I Wonder. An Epitaph	*A Point of View*, BBC Radio 4, 11 September 2022
The Boy Who Would Be King	*Radio Times,* 2 May 2023
Dawn Chorus	*Telegraph,* 2 May 2021
Taking Time	*A Point of View*, BBC Radio 4, 22 December 2023
A Letter from Grandpa Christmas	From 'Grandpa Christmas', Farshore, 2018
Poems for Vivaldi's 'Four Seasons'	Written for a performance at The Southbank Centre with Daniel Pioro on 21 May 2023

ENDNOTES

1 From *Motherland* by Natasha Walter (Copyright © Natasha Walter, 2008) Reproduced by permission of A M Heath & Co. Ltd. Authors' Agents.
2 From *Motherland* by Natasha Walter (Copyright © Natasha Walter, 2008) Reproduced by permission of A M Heath & Co. Ltd. Authors' Agents.
3 From *The Kites Are Flying* by Michael Morpurgo, Walker Books, 2009
4 © Sean Rafferty Estate. Taken from a letter written to friends and supporters of Farms for City Children, 1970s
5 Reproduced with permission from the family of Alexander Gillespie
6 From *I Believe in Unicorns*, Michael Morpurgo, Walker Books, 2015
7 From *My Heart Was a Tree*, Michael Morpurgo, Two Hoots, 2023

INDEX

ageing process 267–71
Alfred the Great 194–5
Amnesty International 96
Anne Frank Foundation speech 164–9
Arnold, Thomas 182
Arthur, King 209–12
Avenger, HMS 127
Aynsley-Green, Al 90–1

Bannister, Roger 180–2, 185–6
Bater, Denis 287
Bayano, HMS 122–3
BBC 199
Bennett, Alan 1
Blake, William 88
Bostock, Sergeant-Major 229
Boy Who Would Be King, The (Morpurgo) 285
Brecht, Bertolt 191, 204
Bridge, Tony (the author's father) 13–15, 16, 18, 166
Brookes, Dr 182
Bryan, Jonathan 247–8
Budgett, Captain 232–3

But My Heart Was a Tree (Morpurgo) 218

Camilla, Queen 283–4
Cammaerts, Francis (the author's uncle) 174–6
Cammaerts, Kippe (the author's mother) 13–14, 16, 18, 21, 37, 133, 166, 200
Cammaerts, Pieter (the author's uncle) 135, 173–4
Caxton, William 196
Chamberlain, Neville 131
Chariots of Fire 184
Charles III, King 280–5
children/childhood
  challenges of 23–9
  and education 39–44, 102–8
  listening to 243–9
  of the author 18–22, 30–8, 133, 170–2, 200, 209–12
  as refugees 88–93, 138–43
    Richard Dimbleby lecture on 86–113
  rights of 86–8

and *Voices of Children* (Morpurgo) 51–79
Children's Words (ed. Morpurgo) 243
Christmas 13, 18–22, 291–8, 299–303
Cohen, Antonia 84
Coram, Thomas 224–5, 227
Coubertin, Pierre de 182–3
Crossley-Holland, Dominic 129
Cunningham, Hugh 51

Dahl, Roald 237
Darwin, Charles 197
Dickens, Charles 106
Dowsett, Mr 33–4
Dubs, Alfred 142
Dunbar, Polly 22

Eagle in the Snow, An (Morpurgo) 128, 133
Edale (steamer) 123
education 39–44, 102–8, 191–208
Elizabeth II, Queen 272–9
Elliott, Marianne 239
Ellis, Wilf 231–2
European Union 149–57
Eye Can Write (Bryan) 248

Farms for City Children 46–50, 112, 231, 280–1

Finding Alfie (Morpurgo) 179
Forman, Justus 125
Foundling Hospital (Coram's Fields) 223–8
'Four Seasons, The' (Morpurgo) 304–12
Frank, Anne 164–5, 167–8

Gaza 9, 94, 96–7, 98–101, 168–9
George VI, King 274
Gillespie, Alexander 146–8
Gillespie, Thomas 146–7
Goetz, Karl 120
Granville, Christine 175
Great Expectations (film) 13, 16, 17
Gulflight, SS 123
Guttmann, Ludwig 185

Hamlet (Shakespeare) 149
Hard Times (Dickens) 106
Hardy, Thomas 295
Heap, Tom 146
Hedred, Mr 256–7
Hepworth, Barbara 265
Heron, Patrick 265
History Boys, The (Bennett) 1
Hitler, Adolf 131
Hogarth, William 224, 225, 226, 227
Holocaust 164–9, 178
Hubbard, Elbert 125

INDEX

Hughes, Ted 30, 49, 237, 292
Hytner, Nicholas 240

I Believe in Unicorns (Morpurgo) 204–8
In the Mouth of the Wolf (Morpurgo) 137
Invention of Childhood, The (Cunningham) 51, 86
Israel 9, 94–8, 168–9

Jackson, Peter 137
Jones, Basil 240
Julius Caesar (Shakespeare) 149

Kennedy, Kathy 241
Kennedy, Mr 256, 262
Kerr, Judith 167, 269–70
'Kindertransport' programme 139–40, 143
Kites Are Flying, The (Morpurgo) 94–6
Kohler, Adrian 240

Lane, Allen 44, 46, 127
Lane, John 127
Lane, Ngaire 188
Lawrence, D. H. 264, 265
Lear, Edward 19
Lebanon 9
Liddell, Eric 184

Listen to the Moon (Morpurgo) 117–19, 127
Little Amal 80–5
Lloyd, Walter 123
lockdown 158–63, 286–90
Lucky Button (Morpurgo) 228
Lusitania sinking 117–27

Macleod, Ian 172–3
Mansfield, Katherine 265
McIndoe, Archibald 172
Morpurgo, Clare (the author's wife) 44–8, 50, 92, 108, 119, 120, 127, 158, 231, 233, 238, 291
Morpurgo, Galtiero 166
Morpurgo, Jack (the author's stepfather) 14, 166
Morpurgo, Michael
  childhood of 18–22, 30–8, 133, 170–2, 200, 209–12, 253–63
  and Farms for City Children 46–50, 231
  heart bypass surgery 3–5
  in lockdown 158–63
  marriage to Clare 44–6
Morpurgo, Pieter (the author's brother) 14, 15, 16, 32, 33, 133
Morris, Tom 238–9
Motherland (Walter) 88–90
Mountbatten, Lord 278

Mozart Question, The (Morpurgo) 167, 178, 304
Mozart, Wolfgang Amadeus 227–8

New Zealand 107

Olympic Games 182–8
Origin of Species, The (Darwin) 197
'Our Tree of Hope' (Morpurgo) 218–22
Owen, Wilfred 179
Owl and the Pussycat, The (Lear) 19
Owl or Pussycat? (Morpurgo) 22

Paine, Thomas 86
Paralympic Games 185
Path of Peace 147–8
Pearce, Eric 171–2
Pioro, Daniel 304
Point of View, A 1, 3, 284
Politics Show, The 88
Pollock, Paul 167
poppies 134–7
Private Peaceful (Morpurgo) 137
Prynne (the author's family dog) 31–2, 35, 36
Puffin Keeper, The (Morpurgo) 266

Rafferty, Peggy 44
Rafferty, Sean 44, 122–13
Rashford, Marcus 187
Ravilious, James 49
Ravilious, Robin 49
Redman, Kate 98
Ree, Harry 174
Refugee Council 142
refugees 80–5, 88–93, 138–43
Rendall, Montague 147
Richard Dimbleby lecture 86–113
Rights of Man (Paine) 86
Robbins, Mr 255
Romeo and Juliet (Shakespeare) 149

Safe Passage 142, 143
Save the Children 97, 168–9
Schwieger, Walther 124, 125–6
Seven Stories 162
Shakespeare, William 149, 197
Skipness, Mr 256, 258
Sleeping Sword, The (Morpurgo) 212
Smith, Rae 239
Song of Gladness (Morpurgo) 288, 289
Spielberg, Steven 241
Stafford, Nick 239
Sullivan, Sir John 227, 228
Sutton, Adrian 239

INDEX

Tams, John 239–40
Tandey, Henry 129–33
They Shall Not Grow Old (film) 137
Thomas, Dylan 37
Thunberg, Greta 245–7
Trojan Wars 212–15
Turner, William 123

United Nations Convention on the Rights of the Child 86–7

Vanderbilt, Alfred 125
Vindication of the Rights of Woman, A (Wollstonecraft) 86
Vivaldi, Antonio 304
Voices of Children (Morpurgo) (radio play) 51–79

Walter, Natasha 88–90
War Horse, The (Morpurgo) 3, 137, 170, 229–42
Ward family 48–9

Weeks, Alfred 234
West Bank 94
When Fishes Flew (Morpurgo) 214–17
When Hitler Stole Pink Rabbit (Kerr) 167
Wherever My Wellies Take Me (Morpurgo & Morpurgo) 50
Why the Whales Came to *The Wreck of the Zanzibar* (Morpurgo) 266
Williamson, Henry 45
Wilson, Emily 215
Windows for Peace 97
Winton, Nicholas 139–40, 167
Wollstonecraft, Mary 86
Wordsworth, William 294

Yarl's Wood 88–90, 91–2, 99, 102
Yousafzai, Malala 245

Zennor 264–6

RAISING READERS
Books Build Bright Futures

Dear Reader,

We'd love your attention for one more page to tell you about the crisis in children's reading, and what we can all do.

Studies have shown that reading for fun is the **single biggest predictor of a child's future success** – more than family circumstances, parents' educational background or income. It improves academic results, mental health, wealth, communication skills, and ambition.

The number of children reading for fun is in rapid decline. Young people have a lot of competition for their time, and a worryingly high number do not have a single book at home.

Our business works extensively with schools, libraries and literacy charities, but here are some ways we can all raise more readers:

- Reading to children for just 10 minutes a day makes a difference
- Don't give up if children aren't regular readers – there will be books for them!
- Visit bookshops and libraries to get recommendations
- Encourage them to listen to audiobooks
- Support school libraries
- Give books as gifts

Thank you for reading: there's a lot more information about how to encourage children to read on our website.

www.JoinRaisingReaders.com